THIS IS YOUR **PASSBOOK**® FOR ...

MEDICAL LABORATORY TECHNICIAN (SUBSTANCE ABUSE)

NLC®

NATIONAL LEARNING CORPORATION®

passbooks.com

Copyright © 2018 by

NLC®
National Learning Corporation

212 Michael Drive, Syosset, NY 11791
(516) 921-8888 • www.passbooks.com
E-mail: info@passbooks.com

PUBLISHED IN THE UNITED STATES OF AMERICA

PASSBOOK® SERIES

THE *PASSBOOK® SERIES* has been created to prepare applicants and candidates for the ultimate academic battlefield – the examination room.

At some time in our lives, each and every one of us may be required to take an examination – for validation, matriculation, admission, qualification, registration, certification, or licensure.

Based on the assumption that every applicant or candidate has met the basic formal educational standards, has taken the required number of courses, and read the necessary texts, the *PASSBOOK® SERIES* furnishes the one special preparation which may assure passing with confidence, instead of failing with insecurity. Examination questions – together with answers – are furnished as the basic vehicle for study so that the mysteries of the examination and its compounding difficulties may be eliminated or diminished by a sure method.

This book is meant to help you pass your examination provided that you qualify and are serious in your objective.

The entire field is reviewed through the huge store of content information which is succinctly presented through a provocative and challenging approach – the question-and-answer method.

A climate of success is established by furnishing the correct answers at the end of each test.

You soon learn to recognize types of questions, forms of questions, and patterns of questioning. You may even begin to anticipate expected outcomes.

You perceive that many questions are repeated or adapted so that you can gain acute insights, which may enable you to score many sure points.

You learn how to confront new questions, or types of questions, and to attack them confidently and work out the correct answers.

You note objectives and emphases, and recognize pitfalls and dangers, so that you may make positive educational adjustments.

Moreover, you are kept fully informed in relation to new concepts, methods, practices, and directions in the field.

You discover that you arre actually taking the examination all the time: you are preparing for the examination by "taking" an examination, not by reading extraneous and/or supererogatory textbooks.

In short, this PASSBOOK®, used directedly, should be an important factor in helping you to pass your test.

MEDICAL LABORATORY TECHNICIAN
(SUBSTANCE ABUSE)

DUTIES
Performs standard laboratory tests on specimens for the analysis and identification of drugs of abuse. The specimens of human tissues and body fluids, primary urine, are analyzed on a large volume basis and occasionally on an emergency basis. Sets up and prepares samples and laboratory equipment for tests used in the analysis for drugs of abuse conducted by other laboratory professional staff. Duties will also include keeping of laboratory records, especially as they related to the specific testing and samples you perform. In addition, you may be responsible for directing the activities of laboratory workers and clerks in addition to technicians and laboratory aides. Your duties as a supervisor, would include: allocating work assignments, evaluating the work performed by assigned staff and when necessary, orientating staff to laboratory procedures, techniques and methods used in the analysis for drugs of abuse.

SUBJECT OF EXAMINATION
Written test designed to test for knowledge, skills, and/or abilities in such areas as:
1. Laboratory principles, procedures, equipment, and terminology;
2. Basic principles of biology, chemistry, and general science;
3. Arithmetic and algebraic reasoning;
4. Analysis for drugs of abuse;
5. Equipment and instrumentation associated with analysis of drugs of abuse;
6. Basic record keeping; and
7. Supervision.

HOW TO TAKE A TEST

I. YOU MUST PASS AN EXAMINATION

A. *WHAT EVERY CANDIDATE SHOULD KNOW*

Examination applicants often ask us for help in preparing for the written test. What can I study in advance? What kinds of questions will be asked? How will the test be given? How will the papers be graded?

As an applicant for a civil service examination, you may be wondering about some of these things. Our purpose here is to suggest effective methods of advance study and to describe civil service examinations.

Your chances for success on this examination can be increased if you know how to prepare. Those "pre-examination jitters" can be reduced if you know what to expect. You can even experience an adventure in good citizenship if you know why civil service exams are given.

B. *WHY ARE CIVIL SERVICE EXAMINATIONS GIVEN?*

Civil service examinations are important to you in two ways. As a citizen, you want public jobs filled by employees who know how to do their work. As a job seeker, you want a fair chance to compete for that job on an equal footing with other candidates. The best-known means of accomplishing this two-fold goal is the competitive examination.

Exams are widely publicized throughout the nation. They may be administered for jobs in federal, state, city, municipal, town or village governments or agencies.

Any citizen may apply, with some limitations, such as the age or residence of applicants. Your experience and education may be reviewed to see whether you meet the requirements for the particular examination. When these requirements exist, they are reasonable and applied consistently to all applicants. Thus, a competitive examination may cause you some uneasiness now, but it is your privilege and safeguard.

C. *HOW ARE CIVIL SERVICE EXAMS DEVELOPED?*

Examinations are carefully written by trained technicians who are specialists in the field known as "psychological measurement," in consultation with recognized authorities in the field of work that the test will cover. These experts recommend the subject matter areas or skills to be tested; only those knowledges or skills important to your success on the job are included. The most reliable books and source materials available are used as references. Together, the experts and technicians judge the difficulty level of the questions.

Test technicians know how to phrase questions so that the problem is clearly stated. Their ethics do not permit "trick" or "catch" questions. Questions may have been tried out on sample groups, or subjected to statistical analysis, to determine their usefulness.

Written tests are often used in combination with performance tests, ratings of training and experience, and oral interviews. All of these measures combine to form the best-known means of finding the right person for the right job.

II. HOW TO PASS THE WRITTEN TEST

A. NATURE OF THE EXAMINATION

To prepare intelligently for civil service examinations, you should know how they differ from school examinations you have taken. In school you were assigned certain definite pages to read or subjects to cover. The examination questions were quite detailed and usually emphasized memory. Civil service exams, on the other hand, try to discover your present ability to perform the duties of a position, plus your potentiality to learn these duties. In other words, a civil service exam attempts to predict how successful you will be. Questions cover such a broad area that they cannot be as minute and detailed as school exam questions.

In the public service similar kinds of work, or positions, are grouped together in one "class." This process is known as *position-classification*. All the positions in a class are paid according to the salary range for that class. One class title covers all of these positions, and they are all tested by the same examination.

B. FOUR BASIC STEPS

1) Study the announcement

How, then, can you know what subjects to study? Our best answer is: "Learn as much as possible about the class of positions for which you've applied." The exam will test the knowledge, skills and abilities needed to do the work.

Your most valuable source of information about the position you want is the official exam announcement. This announcement lists the training and experience qualifications. Check these standards and apply only if you come reasonably close to meeting them.

The brief description of the position in the examination announcement offers some clues to the subjects which will be tested. Think about the job itself. Review the duties in your mind. Can you perform them, or are there some in which you are rusty? Fill in the blank spots in your preparation.

Many jurisdictions preview the written test in the exam announcement by including a section called "Knowledge and Abilities Required," "Scope of the Examination," or some similar heading. Here you will find out specifically what fields will be tested.

2) Review your own background

Once you learn in general what the position is all about, and what you need to know to do the work, ask yourself which subjects you already know fairly well and which need improvement. You may wonder whether to concentrate on improving your strong areas or on building some background in your fields of weakness. When the announcement has specified "some knowledge" or "considerable knowledge," or has used adjectives like "beginning principles of…" or "advanced … methods," you can get a clue as to the number and difficulty of questions to be asked in any given field. More questions, and hence broader coverage, would be included for those subjects which are more important in the work. Now weigh your strengths and weaknesses against the job requirements and prepare accordingly.

3) Determine the level of the position

Another way to tell how intensively you should prepare is to understand the level of the job for which you are applying. Is it the entering level? In other words, is this the position in which beginners in a field of work are hired? Or is it an intermediate or advanced level? Sometimes this is indicated by such words as "Junior" or "Senior" in the class title. Other jurisdictions use Roman numerals to designate the level – Clerk I, Clerk II, for example. The word "Supervisor" sometimes appears in the title. If the level is not indicated by the title, check the description of duties. Will you be working under very close supervision, or will you have responsibility for independent decisions in this work?

4) Choose appropriate study materials

Now that you know the subjects to be examined and the relative amount of each subject to be covered, you can choose suitable study materials. For beginning level jobs, or even advanced ones, if you have a pronounced weakness in some aspect of your training, read a modern, standard textbook in that field. Be sure it is up to date and has general coverage. Such books are normally available at your library, and the librarian will be glad to help you locate one. For entry-level positions, questions of appropriate difficulty are chosen – neither highly advanced questions, nor those too simple. Such questions require careful thought but not advanced training.

If the position for which you are applying is technical or advanced, you will read more advanced, specialized material. If you are already familiar with the basic principles of your field, elementary textbooks would waste your time. Concentrate on advanced textbooks and technical periodicals. Think through the concepts and review difficult problems in your field.

These are all general sources. You can get more ideas on your own initiative, following these leads. For example, training manuals and publications of the government agency which employs workers in your field can be useful, particularly for technical and professional positions. A letter or visit to the government department involved may result in more specific study suggestions, and certainly will provide you with a more definite idea of the exact nature of the position you are seeking.

III. KINDS OF TESTS

Tests are used for purposes other than measuring knowledge and ability to perform specified duties. For some positions, it is equally important to test ability to make adjustments to new situations or to profit from training. In others, basic mental abilities not dependent on information are essential. Questions which test these things may not appear as pertinent to the duties of the position as those which test for knowledge and information. Yet they are often highly important parts of a fair examination. For very general questions, it is almost impossible to help you direct your study efforts. What we can do is to point out some of the more common of these general abilities needed in public service positions and describe some typical questions.

1) General information

Broad, general information has been found useful for predicting job success in some kinds of work. This is tested in a variety of ways, from vocabulary lists to questions about current events. Basic background in some field of work, such as sociology or economics, may be sampled in a group of questions. Often these are principles which have become familiar to most persons through exposure rather than through formal training. It is difficult to advise you how to study for these questions; being alert to the world around you is our best suggestion.

2) Verbal ability

An example of an ability needed in many positions is verbal or language ability. Verbal ability is, in brief, the ability to use and understand words. Vocabulary and grammar tests are typical measures of this ability. Reading comprehension or paragraph interpretation questions are common in many kinds of civil service tests. You are given a paragraph of written material and asked to find its central meaning.

3) Numerical ability

Number skills can be tested by the familiar arithmetic problem, by checking paired lists of numbers to see which are alike and which are different, or by interpreting charts and graphs. In the latter test, a graph may be printed in the test booklet which you are asked to use as the basis for answering questions.

4) Observation

A popular test for law-enforcement positions is the observation test. A picture is shown to you for several minutes, then taken away. Questions about the picture test your ability to observe both details and larger elements.

5) Following directions

In many positions in the public service, the employee must be able to carry out written instructions dependably and accurately. You may be given a chart with several columns, each column listing a variety of information. The questions require you to carry out directions involving the information given in the chart.

6) Skills and aptitudes

Performance tests effectively measure some manual skills and aptitudes. When the skill is one in which you are trained, such as typing or shorthand, you can practice. These tests are often very much like those given in business school or high school courses. For many of the other skills and aptitudes, however, no short-time preparation can be made. Skills and abilities natural to you or that you have developed throughout your lifetime are being tested.

Many of the general questions just described provide all the data needed to answer the questions and ask you to use your reasoning ability to find the answers. Your best preparation for these tests, as well as for tests of facts and ideas, is to be at your physical and mental best. You, no doubt, have your own methods of getting into an exam-taking mood and keeping "in shape." The next section lists some ideas on this subject.

IV. KINDS OF QUESTIONS

Only rarely is the "essay" question, which you answer in narrative form, used in civil service tests. Civil service tests are usually of the short-answer type. Full instructions for answering these questions will be given to you at the examination. But in case this is your first experience with short-answer questions and separate answer sheets, here is what you need to know:

1) Multiple-choice Questions

Most popular of the short-answer questions is the "multiple choice" or "best answer" question. It can be used, for example, to test for factual knowledge, ability to solve problems or judgment in meeting situations found at work.

A multiple-choice question is normally one of three types—

- It can begin with an incomplete statement followed by several possible endings. You are to find the one ending which *best* completes the statement, although some of the others may not be entirely wrong.
- It can also be a complete statement in the form of a question which is answered by choosing one of the statements listed.
- It can be in the form of a problem – again you select the best answer.

Here is an example of a multiple-choice question with a discussion which should give you some clues as to the method for choosing the right answer:

When an employee has a complaint about his assignment, the action which will *best* help him overcome his difficulty is to
- A. discuss his difficulty with his coworkers
- B. take the problem to the head of the organization
- C. take the problem to the person who gave him the assignment
- D. say nothing to anyone about his complaint

In answering this question, you should study each of the choices to find which is best. Consider choice "A" – Certainly an employee may discuss his complaint with fellow employees, but no change or improvement can result, and the complaint remains unresolved. Choice "B" is a poor choice since the head of the organization probably does not know what assignment you have been given, and taking your problem to him is known as "going over the head" of the supervisor. The supervisor, or person who made the assignment, is the person who can clarify it or correct any injustice. Choice "C" is, therefore, correct. To say nothing, as in choice "D," is unwise. Supervisors have and interest in knowing the problems employees are facing, and the employee is seeking a solution to his problem.

2) True/False Questions

The "true/false" or "right/wrong" form of question is sometimes used. Here a complete statement is given. Your job is to decide whether the statement is right or wrong.

SAMPLE: A roaming cell-phone call to a nearby city costs less than a non-roaming call to a distant city.

This statement is wrong, or false, since roaming calls are more expensive.

This is not a complete list of all possible question forms, although most of the others are variations of these common types. You will always get complete directions for answering questions. Be sure you understand *how* to mark your answers – ask questions until you do.

V. RECORDING YOUR ANSWERS

Computer terminals are used more and more today for many different kinds of exams.

For an examination with very few applicants, you may be told to record your answers in the test booklet itself. Separate answer sheets are much more common. If this separate answer sheet is to be scored by machine – and this is often the case – it is highly important that you mark your answers correctly in order to get credit.

An electronic scoring machine is often used in civil service offices because of the speed with which papers can be scored. Machine-scored answer sheets must be marked with a pencil, which will be given to you. This pencil has a high graphite content which responds to the electronic scoring machine. As a matter of fact, stray dots may register as answers, so do not let your pencil rest on the answer sheet while you are pondering the correct answer. Also, if your pencil lead breaks or is otherwise defective, ask for another.

Since the answer sheet will be dropped in a slot in the scoring machine, be careful not to bend the corners or get the paper crumpled.

The answer sheet normally has five vertical columns of numbers, with 30 numbers to a column. These numbers correspond to the question numbers in your test booklet. After each number, going across the page are four or five pairs of dotted lines. These short dotted lines have small letters or numbers above them. The first two pairs may also have a "T" or "F" above the letters. This indicates that the first two pairs only are to be used if the questions are of the true-false type. If the questions are multiple choice, disregard the "T" and "F" and pay attention only to the small letters or numbers.

Answer your questions in the manner of the sample that follows:

32. The largest city in the United States is
    A. Washington, D.C.
    B. New York City
    C. Chicago
    D. Detroit
    E. San Francisco

1) Choose the answer you think is best. (New York City is the largest, so "B" is correct.)
2) Find the row of dotted lines numbered the same as the question you are answering. (Find row number 32)
3) Find the pair of dotted lines corresponding to the answer. (Find the pair of lines under the mark "B.")
4) Make a solid black mark between the dotted lines.

VI. BEFORE THE TEST

Common sense will help you find procedures to follow to get ready for an examination. Too many of us, however, overlook these sensible measures. Indeed, nervousness and fatigue have been found to be the most serious reasons why applicants fail to do their best on civil service tests. Here is a list of reminders:

- Begin your preparation early – Don't wait until the last minute to go scurrying around for books and materials or to find out what the position is all about.
- Prepare continuously – An hour a night for a week is better than an all-night cram session. This has been definitely established. What is more, a night a week for a month will return better dividends than crowding your study into a shorter period of time.
- Locate the place of the exam – You have been sent a notice telling you when and where to report for the examination. If the location is in a different town or otherwise unfamiliar to you, it would be well to inquire the best route and learn something about the building.
- Relax the night before the test – Allow your mind to rest. Do not study at all that night. Plan some mild recreation or diversion; then go to bed early and get a good night's sleep.
- Get up early enough to make a leisurely trip to the place for the test – This way unforeseen events, traffic snarls, unfamiliar buildings, etc. will not upset you.
- Dress comfortably – A written test is not a fashion show. You will be known by number and not by name, so wear something comfortable.
- Leave excess paraphernalia at home – Shopping bags and odd bundles will get in your way. You need bring only the items mentioned in the official notice you received; usually everything you need is provided. Do not bring reference books to the exam. They will only confuse those last minutes and be taken away from you when in the test room.
- Arrive somewhat ahead of time – If because of transportation schedules you must get there very early, bring a newspaper or magazine to take your mind off yourself while waiting.
- Locate the examination room – When you have found the proper room, you will be directed to the seat or part of the room where you will sit. Sometimes you are given a sheet of instructions to read while you are waiting. Do not fill out any forms until you are told to do so; just read them and be prepared.
- Relax and prepare to listen to the instructions
- If you have any physical problem that may keep you from doing your best, be sure to tell the test administrator. If you are sick or in poor health, you really cannot do your best on the exam. You can come back and take the test some other time.

VII. AT THE TEST

The day of the test is here and you have the test booklet in your hand. The temptation to get going is very strong. Caution! There is more to success than knowing the right answers. You must know how to identify your papers and understand variations in the type of short-answer question used in this particular examination. Follow these suggestions for maximum results from your efforts:

1) Cooperate with the monitor

The test administrator has a duty to create a situation in which you can be as much at ease as possible. He will give instructions, tell you when to begin, check to see that you are marking your answer sheet correctly, and so on. He is not there to guard you, although he will see that your competitors do not take unfair advantage. He wants to help you do your best.

2) Listen to all instructions

Don't jump the gun! Wait until you understand all directions. In most civil service tests you get more time than you need to answer the questions. So don't be in a hurry. Read each word of instructions until you clearly understand the meaning. Study the examples, listen to all announcements and follow directions. Ask questions if you do not understand what to do.

3) Identify your papers

Civil service exams are usually identified by number only. You will be assigned a number; you must not put your name on your test papers. Be sure to copy your number correctly. Since more than one exam may be given, copy your exact examination title.

4) Plan your time

Unless you are told that a test is a "speed" or "rate of work" test, speed itself is usually not important. Time enough to answer all the questions will be provided, but this does not mean that you have all day. An overall time limit has been set. Divide the total time (in minutes) by the number of questions to determine the approximate time you have for each question.

5) Do not linger over difficult questions

If you come across a difficult question, mark it with a paper clip (useful to have along) and come back to it when you have been through the booklet. One caution if you do this – be sure to skip a number on your answer sheet as well. Check often to be sure that you have not lost your place and that you are marking in the row numbered the same as the question you are answering.

6) Read the questions

Be sure you know what the question asks! Many capable people are unsuccessful because they failed to *read* the questions correctly.

7) Answer all questions

Unless you have been instructed that a penalty will be deducted for incorrect answers, it is better to guess than to omit a question.

8) Speed tests

It is often better NOT to guess on speed tests. It has been found that on timed tests people are tempted to spend the last few seconds before time is called in marking answers at random – without even reading them – in the hope of picking up a few extra points. To discourage this practice, the instructions may warn you that your score will be "corrected" for guessing. That is, a penalty will be applied. The incorrect answers will be deducted from the correct ones, or some other penalty formula will be used.

9) Review your answers

If you finish before time is called, go back to the questions you guessed or omitted to give them further thought. Review other answers if you have time.

10) Return your test materials

If you are ready to leave before others have finished or time is called, take ALL your materials to the monitor and leave quietly. Never take any test material with you. The monitor can discover whose papers are not complete, and taking a test booklet may be grounds for disqualification.

VIII. EXAMINATION TECHNIQUES

1) Read the general instructions carefully. These are usually printed on the first page of the exam booklet. As a rule, these instructions refer to the timing of the examination; the fact that you should not start work until the signal and must stop work at a signal, etc. If there are any *special* instructions, such as a choice of questions to be answered, make sure that you note this instruction carefully.

2) When you are ready to start work on the examination, that is as soon as the signal has been given, read the instructions to each question booklet, underline any key words or phrases, such as *least, best, outline, describe* and the like. In this way you will tend to answer as requested rather than discover on reviewing your paper that you *listed without describing*, that you selected the *worst* choice rather than the *best* choice, etc.

3) If the examination is of the objective or multiple-choice type – that is, each question will also give a series of possible answers: A, B, C or D, and you are called upon to select the best answer and write the letter next to that answer on your answer paper – it is advisable to start answering each question in turn. There may be anywhere from 50 to 100 such questions in the three or four hours allotted and you can see how much time would be taken if you read through all the questions before beginning to answer any. Furthermore, if you come across a question or group of questions which you know would be difficult to answer, it would undoubtedly affect your handling of all the other questions.

4) If the examination is of the essay type and contains but a few questions, it is a moot point as to whether you should read all the questions before starting to answer any one. Of course, if you are given a choice – say five out of seven and the like – then it is essential to read all the questions so you can eliminate the two that are most difficult. If, however, you are asked to answer all the questions, there may be danger in trying to answer the easiest one first because you may find that you will spend too much time on it. The best technique is to answer the first question, then proceed to the second, etc.

5) Time your answers. Before the exam begins, write down the time it started, then add the time allowed for the examination and write down the time it must be completed, then divide the time available somewhat as follows:

- If 3-1/2 hours are allowed, that would be 210 minutes. If you have 80 objective-type questions, that would be an average of 2-1/2 minutes per question. Allow yourself no more than 2 minutes per question, or a total of 160 minutes, which will permit about 50 minutes to review.
- If for the time allotment of 210 minutes there are 7 essay questions to answer, that would average about 30 minutes a question. Give yourself only 25 minutes per question so that you have about 35 minutes to review.

6) The most important instruction is to *read each question* and make sure you know what is wanted. The second most important instruction is to *time yourself properly* so that you answer every question. The third most important instruction is to *answer every question*. Guess if you have to but include something for each question. Remember that you will receive no credit for a blank and will probably receive some credit if you write something in answer to an essay question. If you guess a letter – say "B" for a multiple-choice question – you may have guessed right. If you leave a blank as an answer to a multiple-choice question, the examiners may respect your feelings but it will not add a point to your score. Some exams may penalize you for wrong answers, so in such cases *only*, you may not want to guess unless you have some basis for your answer.

7) Suggestions
   a. Objective-type questions
      1. Examine the question booklet for proper sequence of pages and questions
      2. Read all instructions carefully
      3. Skip any question which seems too difficult; return to it after all other questions have been answered
      4. Apportion your time properly; do not spend too much time on any single question or group of questions
      5. Note and underline key words – *all, most, fewest, least, best, worst, same, opposite,* etc.
      6. Pay particular attention to negatives
      7. Note unusual option, e.g., unduly long, short, complex, different or similar in content to the body of the question
      8. Observe the use of "hedging" words – *probably, may, most likely,* etc.
      9. Make sure that your answer is put next to the same number as the question
      10. Do not second-guess unless you have good reason to believe the second answer is definitely more correct
      11. Cross out original answer if you decide another answer is more accurate; do not erase until you are ready to hand your paper in
      12. Answer all questions; guess unless instructed otherwise
      13. Leave time for review

   b. Essay questions
      1. Read each question carefully
      2. Determine exactly what is wanted. Underline key words or phrases.
      3. Decide on outline or paragraph answer

4. Include many different points and elements unless asked to develop any one or two points or elements
5. Show impartiality by giving pros and cons unless directed to select one side only
6. Make and write down any assumptions you find necessary to answer the questions
7. Watch your English, grammar, punctuation and choice of words
8. Time your answers; don't crowd material

8) Answering the essay question

Most essay questions can be answered by framing the specific response around several key words or ideas. Here are a few such key words or ideas:

M's: manpower, materials, methods, money, management
P's: purpose, program, policy, plan, procedure, practice, problems, pitfalls, personnel, public relations
   a. Six basic steps in handling problems:
       1. Preliminary plan and background development
       2. Collect information, data and facts
       3. Analyze and interpret information, data and facts
       4. Analyze and develop solutions as well as make recommendations
       5. Prepare report and sell recommendations
       6. Install recommendations and follow up effectiveness

   b. Pitfalls to avoid
       1. *Taking things for granted* – A statement of the situation does not necessarily imply that each of the elements is necessarily true; for example, a complaint may be invalid and biased so that all that can be taken for granted is that a complaint has been registered
       2. *Considering only one side of a situation* – Wherever possible, indicate several alternatives and then point out the reasons you selected the best one
       3. *Failing to indicate follow up* – Whenever your answer indicates action on your part, make certain that you will take proper follow-up action to see how successful your recommendations, procedures or actions turn out to be
       4. *Taking too long in answering any single question* – Remember to time your answers properly

IX. AFTER THE TEST

Scoring procedures differ in detail among civil service jurisdictions although the general principles are the same. Whether the papers are hand-scored or graded by machine we have described, they are nearly always graded by number. That is, the person who marks the paper knows only the number – never the name – of the applicant. Not until all the papers have been graded will they be matched with names. If other tests, such as training and experience or oral interview ratings have been given, scores will be combined. Different parts of the examination usually have different weights. For example, the written test might count 60 percent of the final grade, and a rating of training and experience 40 percent. In many jurisdictions, veterans will have a certain number of points added to their grades.

After the final grade has been determined, the names are placed in grade order and an eligible list is established. There are various methods for resolving ties between those who get the same final grade – probably the most common is to place first the name of the person whose application was received first. Job offers are made from the eligible list in the order the names appear on it. You will be notified of your grade and your rank as soon as all these computations have been made. This will be done as rapidly as possible.

People who are found to meet the requirements in the announcement are called "eligibles." Their names are put on a list of eligible candidates. An eligible's chances of getting a job depend on how high he stands on this list and how fast agencies are filling jobs from the list.

When a job is to be filled from a list of eligibles, the agency asks for the names of people on the list of eligibles for that job. When the civil service commission receives this request, it sends to the agency the names of the three people highest on this list. Or, if the job to be filled has specialized requirements, the office sends the agency the names of the top three persons who meet these requirements from the general list.

The appointing officer makes a choice from among the three people whose names were sent to him. If the selected person accepts the appointment, the names of the others are put back on the list to be considered for future openings.

That is the rule in hiring from all kinds of eligible lists, whether they are for typist, carpenter, chemist, or something else. For every vacancy, the appointing officer has his choice of any one of the top three eligibles on the list. This explains why the person whose name is on top of the list sometimes does not get an appointment when some of the persons lower on the list do. If the appointing officer chooses the second or third eligible, the No. 1 eligible does not get a job at once, but stays on the list until he is appointed or the list is terminated.

X. HOW TO PASS THE INTERVIEW TEST

The examination for which you applied requires an oral interview test. You have already taken the written test and you are now being called for the interview test – the final part of the formal examination.

You may think that it is not possible to prepare for an interview test and that there are no procedures to follow during an interview. Our purpose is to point out some things you can do in advance that will help you and some good rules to follow and pitfalls to avoid while you are being interviewed.

What is an interview supposed to test?
The written examination is designed to test the technical knowledge and competence of the candidate; the oral is designed to evaluate intangible qualities, not readily measured otherwise, and to establish a list showing the relative fitness of each candidate – as measured against his competitors – for the position sought. Scoring is not on the basis of "right" and "wrong," but on a sliding scale of values ranging from "not passable" to "outstanding." As a matter of fact, it is possible to achieve a relatively low score without a single "incorrect" answer because of evident weakness in the qualities being measured.

Occasionally, an examination may consist entirely of an oral test – either an individual or a group oral. In such cases, information is sought concerning the technical knowledges and abilities of the candidate, since there has been no written examination for this purpose. More commonly, however, an oral test is used to supplement a written examination.

Who conducts interviews?

The composition of oral boards varies among different jurisdictions. In nearly all, a representative of the personnel department serves as chairman. One of the members of the board may be a representative of the department in which the candidate would work. In some cases, "outside experts" are used, and, frequently, a businessman or some other representative of the general public is asked to serve. Labor and management or other special groups may be represented. The aim is to secure the services of experts in the appropriate field.

However the board is composed, it is a good idea (and not at all improper or unethical) to ascertain in advance of the interview who the members are and what groups they represent. When you are introduced to them, you will have some idea of their backgrounds and interests, and at least you will not stutter and stammer over their names.

What should be done before the interview?

While knowledge about the board members is useful and takes some of the surprise element out of the interview, there is other preparation which is more substantive. It *is* possible to prepare for an oral interview – in several ways:

1) Keep a copy of your application and review it carefully before the interview

This may be the only document before the oral board, and the starting point of the interview. Know what education and experience you have listed there, and the sequence and dates of all of it. Sometimes the board will ask you to review the highlights of your experience for them; you should not have to hem and haw doing it.

2) Study the class specification and the examination announcement

Usually, the oral board has one or both of these to guide them. The qualities, characteristics or knowledges required by the position sought are stated in these documents. They offer valuable clues as to the nature of the oral interview. For example, if the job involves supervisory responsibilities, the announcement will usually indicate that knowledge of modern supervisory methods and the qualifications of the candidate as a supervisor will be tested. If so, you can expect such questions, frequently in the form of a hypothetical situation which you are expected to solve. NEVER go into an oral without knowledge of the duties and responsibilities of the job you seek.

3) Think through each qualification required

Try to visualize the kind of questions you would ask if you were a board member. How well could you answer them? Try especially to appraise your own knowledge and background in each area, *measured against the job sought*, and identify any areas in which you are weak. Be critical and realistic – do not flatter yourself.

4) Do some general reading in areas in which you feel you may be weak

For example, if the job involves supervision and your past experience has NOT, some general reading in supervisory methods and practices, particularly in the field of human relations, might be useful. Do NOT study agency procedures or detailed manuals. The oral board will be testing your understanding and capacity, not your memory.

5) Get a good night's sleep and watch your general health and mental attitude

You will want a clear head at the interview. Take care of a cold or any other minor ailment, and of course, no hangovers.

What should be done on the day of the interview?

Now comes the day of the interview itself. Give yourself plenty of time to get there. Plan to arrive somewhat ahead of the scheduled time, particularly if your appointment is in the fore part of the day. If a previous candidate fails to appear, the board might be ready for you a bit early. By early afternoon an oral board is almost invariably behind schedule if there are many candidates, and you may have to wait. Take along a book or magazine to read, or your application to review, but leave any extraneous material in the waiting room when you go in for your interview. In any event, relax and compose yourself.

The matter of dress is important. The board is forming impressions about you – from your experience, your manners, your attitude, and your appearance. Give your personal appearance careful attention. Dress your best, but not your flashiest. Choose conservative, appropriate clothing, and be sure it is immaculate. This is a business interview, and your appearance should indicate that you regard it as such. Besides, being well groomed and properly dressed will help boost your confidence.

Sooner or later, someone will call your name and escort you into the interview room. *This is it.* From here on you are on your own. It is too late for any more preparation. But remember, you asked for this opportunity to prove your fitness, and you are here because your request was granted.

What happens when you go in?

The usual sequence of events will be as follows: The clerk (who is often the board stenographer) will introduce you to the chairman of the oral board, who will introduce you to the other members of the board. Acknowledge the introductions before you sit down. Do not be surprised if you find a microphone facing you or a stenotypist sitting by. Oral interviews are usually recorded in the event of an appeal or other review.

Usually the chairman of the board will open the interview by reviewing the highlights of your education and work experience from your application – primarily for the benefit of the other members of the board, as well as to get the material into the record. Do not interrupt or comment unless there is an error or significant misinterpretation; if that is the case, do not hesitate. But do not quibble about insignificant matters. Also, he will usually ask you some question about your education, experience or your present job – partly to get you to start talking and to establish the interviewing "rapport." He may start the actual questioning, or turn it over to one of the other members. Frequently, each member undertakes the questioning on a particular area, one in which he is perhaps most competent, so you can expect each member to participate in the examination. Because time is limited, you may also expect some rather abrupt switches in the direction the questioning takes, so do not be upset by it. Normally, a board member will not pursue a single line of questioning unless he discovers a particular strength or weakness.

After each member has participated, the chairman will usually ask whether any member has any further questions, then will ask you if you have anything you wish to add. Unless you are expecting this question, it may floor you. Worse, it may start you off on an extended, extemporaneous speech. The board is not usually seeking more information. The question is principally to offer you a last opportunity to present further qualifications or to indicate that you have nothing to add. So, if you feel that a significant qualification or characteristic has been overlooked, it is proper to point it out in a sentence or so. Do not compliment the board on the thoroughness of their examination – they have been sketchy, and you know it. If you wish, merely say, "No thank you, I have nothing further to add." This is a point where you can "talk yourself out" of a good impression or fail to present an important bit of information. Remember, *you close the interview yourself.*

The chairman will then say, "That is all, Mr. _____, thank you." Do not be startled; the interview is over, and quicker than you think. Thank him, gather your belongings and take your leave. Save your sigh of relief for the other side of the door.

How to put your best foot forward

Throughout this entire process, you may feel that the board individually and collectively is trying to pierce your defenses, seek out your hidden weaknesses and embarrass and confuse you. Actually, this is not true. They are obliged to make an appraisal of your qualifications for the job you are seeking, and they want to see you in your best light. Remember, they must interview all candidates and a non-cooperative candidate may become a failure in spite of their best efforts to bring out his qualifications. Here are 15 suggestions that will help you:

1) Be natural – Keep your attitude confident, not cocky

If you are not confident that you can do the job, do not expect the board to be. Do not apologize for your weaknesses, try to bring out your strong points. The board is interested in a positive, not negative, presentation. Cockiness will antagonize any board member and make him wonder if you are covering up a weakness by a false show of strength.

2) Get comfortable, but don't lounge or sprawl

Sit erectly but not stiffly. A careless posture may lead the board to conclude that you are careless in other things, or at least that you are not impressed by the importance of the occasion. Either conclusion is natural, even if incorrect. Do not fuss with your clothing, a pencil or an ashtray. Your hands may occasionally be useful to emphasize a point; do not let them become a point of distraction.

3) Do not wisecrack or make small talk

This is a serious situation, and your attitude should show that you consider it as such. Further, the time of the board is limited – they do not want to waste it, and neither should you.

4) Do not exaggerate your experience or abilities

In the first place, from information in the application or other interviews and sources, the board may know more about you than you think. Secondly, you probably will not get away with it. An experienced board is rather adept at spotting such a situation, so do not take the chance.

5) If you know a board member, do not make a point of it, yet do not hide it

Certainly you are not fooling him, and probably not the other members of the board. Do not try to take advantage of your acquaintanceship – it will probably do you little good.

6) Do not dominate the interview

Let the board do that. They will give you the clues – do not assume that you have to do all the talking. Realize that the board has a number of questions to ask you, and do not try to take up all the interview time by showing off your extensive knowledge of the answer to the first one.

7) Be attentive

You only have 20 minutes or so, and you should keep your attention at its sharpest throughout. When a member is addressing a problem or question to you, give him your undivided attention. Address your reply principally to him, but do not exclude the other board members.

8) Do not interrupt

A board member may be stating a problem for you to analyze. He will ask you a question when the time comes. Let him state the problem, and wait for the question.

9) Make sure you understand the question

Do not try to answer until you are sure what the question is. If it is not clear, restate it in your own words or ask the board member to clarify it for you. However, do not haggle about minor elements.

10) Reply promptly but not hastily

A common entry on oral board rating sheets is "candidate responded readily," or "candidate hesitated in replies." Respond as promptly and quickly as you can, but do not jump to a hasty, ill-considered answer.

11) Do not be peremptory in your answers

A brief answer is proper – but do not fire your answer back. That is a losing game from your point of view. The board member can probably ask questions much faster than you can answer them.

12) Do not try to create the answer you think the board member wants

He is interested in what kind of mind you have and how it works – not in playing games. Furthermore, he can usually spot this practice and will actually grade you down on it.

13) Do not switch sides in your reply merely to agree with a board member

Frequently, a member will take a contrary position merely to draw you out and to see if you are willing and able to defend your point of view. Do not start a debate, yet do not surrender a good position. If a position is worth taking, it is worth defending.

14) Do not be afraid to admit an error in judgment if you are shown to be wrong

The board knows that you are forced to reply without any opportunity for careful consideration. Your answer may be demonstrably wrong. If so, admit it and get on with the interview.

15) Do not dwell at length on your present job

The opening question may relate to your present assignment. Answer the question but do not go into an extended discussion. You are being examined for a *new* job, not your present one. As a matter of fact, try to phrase ALL your answers in terms of the job for which you are being examined.

Basis of Rating

Probably you will forget most of these "do's" and "don'ts" when you walk into the oral interview room. Even remembering them all will not ensure you a passing grade. Perhaps you did not have the qualifications in the first place. But remembering them will help you to put your best foot forward, without treading on the toes of the board members.

Rumor and popular opinion to the contrary notwithstanding, an oral board wants you to make the best appearance possible. They know you are under pressure – but they also want to see how you respond to it as a guide to what your reaction would be under the pressures of the job you seek. They will be influenced by the degree of poise you display, the personal traits you show and the manner in which you respond.

ABOUT THIS BOOK

This book contains tests divided into Examination Sections. Go through each test, answering every question in the margin. At the end of each test look at the answer key and check your answers. On the ones you got wrong, look at the right answer choice and learn. Do not fill in the answers first. Do not memorize the questions and answers, but understand the answer and principles involved. On your test, the questions will likely be different from the samples. Questions are changed and new ones added. If you understand these past questions you should have success with any changes that arise. Tests may consist of several types of questions. We have additional books on each subject should more study be advisable or necessary for you. Finally, the more you study, the better prepared you will be. This book is intended to be the last thing you study before you walk into the examination room. Prior study of relevant texts is also recommended. NLC publishes some of these in our Fundamental Series. Knowledge and good sense are important factors in passing your exam. Good luck also helps. So now study this Passbook, absorb the material contained within and take that knowledge into the examination. Then do your best to pass that exam.

———

EXAMINATION SECTION

EXAMINATION SECTION
TEST 1

DIRECTIONS: Each question or incomplete statement is followed by several suggested answers or completions. Select the one that BEST answers the question or completes the statement. *PRINT THE LETTER OF THE CORRECT ANSWER IN THE SPACE AT THE RIGHT.*

1. After extensive use of the oil immersion lens of a compound microscope, xylol should be used to clean the

    A. condenser lens
    C. eyepiece
    B. objective lens
    D. iris diaphragm

1.____

2. When using a compound microscope, it is necessary to focus light on the object by use of the

    A. condenser lens
    C. eyepiece
    B. objective lens
    D. iris diaphragm

2.____

3. Polarizing microscopes, phase contrast microscopes, and interference microscopes differ from the standard compound light microscope in that they all use a different type of

    A. light source
    C. objective lens
    B. condenser lens
    D. eyepiece

3.____

4. The amount of light used to view an object with a compound microscope CANNOT be varied by changing the adjustment of the

    A. Kohler illuminator
    C. condenser lens
    B. iris diaphragm
    D. binocular eyepiece

4.____

5. When not in use, the beam and pan supports of an analytical balance should be elevated so as to

    A. prevent injury to the knife edges
    B. keep the balance level
    C. prevent dust from entering the mechanism
    D. keep the balance at a zero reading

5.____

6. Assume that you are weighing a powder on an analytical balance with a direct-reading scale. You place a beaker on the pan and determine that the beaker weighs 13.854 grams. After adding the powder to the beaker, the readings on the balance knobs show: 100 gram - 0; 10 gram - 30; and 1 gram - 8.
The 0 mark on the Vernier scale is between 85 and 86, and the 3rd mark up on the Vernier coincides with a mark on the general scale.
The weight of the powder is _____ grams.

    A. 13.854   B. 24.999   C. 38.853   D. 52.707

6.____

7. Which is the LEAST common blood type among the major blood groups?

    A. A   B. B   C. AB   D. O

7.____

1

8. The one of the following instruments which is NOT used to measure specific gravity of a liquid is called a   8.____

    A. hydrometer   B. urinometer
    C. lactometer   D. hygrometer

9. A microhemocrit test is performed and it is noted that the packed erythrocytes make up about 1/5th of the total volume of blood in the tube.   9.____
The number of erythrocytes found in this patient is APPROXIMATELY what percentage of the number normally found?

    A. 20   B. 50   C. 80   D. 100

10. The normal specific gravity of urine is APPROXIMATELY   10.____

    A. 1.000   B. 1.020   C. 1.050   D. 1.100

11. When not in immediate or constant use, the electrodes of a pH meter should be   11.____

    A. stored in a refrigerator
    B. kept immersed in distilled water
    C. kept immersed in normal saline
    D. dried and the fluid emptied from inside the electrode

12. The normal pH of blood is about 7.4.   12.____
This means that blood is

    A. strongly acidic   B. very slightly acidic
    C. exactly neutral   D. very slightly alkaline

13. Proper use of a clinical centrifuge includes   13.____

    A. balancing the tubes that are placed in the rotor
    B. keeping the top open when in use
    C. immediately turning to the top required speed
    D. using any available test tube for the sample

14. When using a spectrophotometer, which one of the following will result in errors in the results?   14.____

    A. Cuvet covers being used
    B. Cuvets being wiped clean of dirt and fingerprints
    C. Solutions used being turbid
    D. Color development being carried out at identical times and temperatures

15. You are required to determine the amount of glucose in a blood sample. 100 ml of a standard solution was made up containing 100 mg of glucose, and 100 ml of serum was provided. Ten ml of each was used to carry out a benedict"s test, and the results were read in a spectrophotometer. The optical density reading of the standard was 0.200, and the serum sample was 0.150.   15.____
What was the amount of glucose in the total blood sample?
_____ mg.

    A. 13.3   B. 133   C. 150   D. 200

16. Which one of the following solutions has the LOWEST pH? 1 N _____.   16.____

    A. HCl   B. acetic acid
    C. ammonium hydroxide   D. NaOH

17. Which one of the following solutions has the HIGHEST pH? 1 N _____.   17.____

    A. HCl   B. acetic acid
    C. ammonium hydroxide   D. NaOH

18. What is the molecular weight of oxygen?   18.____

    A. 1   B. 8   C. 16   D. 40

19. A molar solution of a compound is one that contains one gram _____ of solution.   19.____

    A. molecular weight of the compound per 100 ml
    B. molecular weight of the compound per liter
    C. of the compound per 100 ml
    D. of the compound per liter

20. The SECOND reagent, and the time required for the reagent that is added to a slide   20.____
when preparing a gram stain, is

    A. crystal violet (gentian violet) for 1 minute
    B. iodine for 1 minute
    C. safranin for 1 minute
    D. safranin for 20 to 30 seconds

21. The BEST staining procedure for the identification of Mycobacterium tuberculosis would   21.____
be the _____ stain.

    A. gram   B. acid-fast   C. spore   D. capsule

22. Identification of filamentous fungi is *usually* based on the   22.____

    A. shape and arrangement of the spores
    B. hemolysis on blood agar plates
    C. fermentation of various sugars
    D. reaction on a TSI slant

23. Which species of bacteria would be the LEAST likely to be killed by boiling in water for 15   23.____
minutes?

    A. Staphylococcus   B. Escherichia
    C. Clostridium   D. Streptococcus

24. A gram stain of a streptococcus, when observed under the oil immersion lens of a micro-   24.____
scope, will be

    A. pink-colored cocci in chains
    B. blue-colored rods
    C. blue-colored cocci in grape-like clusters
    D. blue-colored cocci in chains

25. The MOST numerous of the white blood cells is the   25._____

    A. eosinophil   B. neutraphil
    C. lymphocyte   D. basophil

KEY (CORRECT ANSWERS)

1.	B		11.	B
2.	A		12.	D
3.	B		13.	A
4.	D		14.	C
5.	A		15.	B
6.	B		16.	A
7.	C		17.	D
8.	D		18.	C
9.	B		19.	B
10.	B		20.	B

21.	B
22.	A
23.	C
24.	D
25.	B

TEST 2

DIRECTIONS: Each question or incomplete statement is followed by several suggested answers or completions. Select the one that BEST answers the question or completes the statement. *PRINT THE LETTER OF THE CORRECT ANSWER IN THE SPACE AT THE RIGHT.*

1. Which one of the following chemicals is NOT flammable and can be used if there is a bunsen burner lit in the room?

    A. Amyl alcohol   B. Potassium hydroxide
    C. Benzene   D. Xylene

1.____

2. A water or soda-type of fire extinguisher should NEVER be used to extinguish a fire in which there is

    A. alcohol
    B. paper
    C. an electrical short-circuit
    D. methanol

2.____

3. The amount of solids in 1000 ml of urine may be estimated by multiplying the last two figures of the specific gravity by 2.6.
If a given sample of urine has a specific gravity of 1.020, about how many grams of solid are there in 1500 ml of that urine sample?
_____ grams.

    A. 39   B. 52   C. 78   D. 260

3.____

4. If 17.3 grams of copper sulfate are required to make 1 liter of Benedict's solution, how much copper sulfate would be needed to make 350 ml of the solution?
_____ grams.

    A. 1.73   B. 6.06   C. 17.3   D. 35.0

4.____

5. 25° Centigrade MOST closely approximates which one of the following temperatures?

    A. Room temperature
    B. Body temperature
    C. Refrigerator temperature
    D. The freezing temperature of water

5.____

6. One ml of blood is diluted in 99 ml of saline. There are 50,000 red blood cells in 1 ml of this suspension. The red cell count of the blood per ml is

    A. 503   B. 5000   C. 5×10^6 D. 50×10^3

6.____

7. A patient who has fasted overnight is given a solution of sugar, and his blood specimens are tested at half-hour or hourly intervals to determine the amount of sugar in the blood. This test is called a

    A. GTT   B. hematocrit
    C. CBC   D. 2 hr P.P.

7.____

9. A stain that would be useful in identifying starch granules in urine is   9.____

    A. gram stain   B. iodine
    C. sudan III   D. benzidine nitroprusside

10. A biological substance that *increases* the rate of a chemical reaction is a(n)   10.____

    A. buffer   B. enzyme
    C. centrifuge   D. solvent

11. A measurement of the density of a solution as compared with the density of water is called   11.____

    A. specific gravity   B. specific conductance
    C. titration   D. optical density

12. A substance that is added to a chemical reaction to prevent a large change in pH is a(n)   12.____

    A. enzyme   B. indicator   C. buffer   D. isotope

13. Which one of the following chemicals is NOT a pH indicator?   13.____

    A. Phenolphthalein   B. Methyl red
    C. Methylene blue   D. Brilliant yellow

14. The Clinitest® sugar test, used to show the amount of glucose in urine, is the *same* type of test as   14.____

    A. the Benedict's test   B. the Biuret test
    C. Test-tape®   D. the Kahn test

15. All of the following are lipids EXCEPT   15.____

    A. cholesterol   B. albumin
    C. olive oil   D. lecithin

Questions 16-20.

DIRECTIONS: Questions 16 through 20 are to be answered SOLELY on the basis of the chart shown on the next page.

QUARTERLY CLINIC WORKLOAD REPORT
LABORATORIES X, Y, Z
SECOND QUARTER, 2003 AND 2004

Tests Performed	2004			2003		
	April	May	June	April	May	June
LABORATORY X Hematocrit	175	142	164	181	147	153
Urine	502	554	495	659	575	532
Sickle cells	61	85	80	54	91	74
White blood count	5	10	7	11	26	15
Hemoglobin	14	12	16	9	18	16
Pregnancy tests	203	186	214	189	207	196
Total Examinations	960	989	976	1103	1064	986
RH and STS sent to Worth St.	306	299	239	407	338	287
Tests performed by other agencies	292	313	302	356	391	333
Total Tests Sent Out	598	612	541	763	729	620
LABORATORY Y						
Hematocrit	203	157	192	147	162	198
Urine	476	516	447	386	409	422
Sickle cells	78	49	63	45	53	47
White blood count	13	7	9	16	18	13
Hemoglobin	16	19	23	14	14	9
Pregnancy tests	142	186	197	153	204	216
Total Examinations						
RH and STS sent to Worth St.	287	312	314	272	306	315
Tests performed by other agencies	323	216	254	310	381	326
Total Tests Sent Out	610	528	568	582	687	641
LABORATORY Z						
Hematocrit	203	177	184	213	201	174
Urine	452	505	478	491	349	379
Sickle cells	67	54	49	58	37	46
White blood count	11	13	14	21	10	17
Hemoglobin	19	22	24	16	17	12
Pregnancy tests	218	182	216	165	175	184
Total Examinations	970	953	965	964	789	812
RH and STS sent to Worth St.	272	298	317	314	288	303
Tests performed by other agencies	314	335	298	347	228	332
Total Tests Sent Out	586	633	615	661	516	635

16. The difference between the total examinations performed in Laboratory Y in May 2004   16.____
    and May 2003 is

     A.   26   B.   68   C.   74   D.   167

17. In which of the following laboratories and years was the GREATEST number of urine   17.____
    tests for the months of April, May, and June performed?
    Laboratory

     A.   Y in 2003   B.   Y in 2004
     C.   X in 2003   D.   X in 2004

18. White blood count tests comprise APPROXIMATELY what percentage of the total num-   18.____
    ber of examinations performed?

     A.   1%   B.   5%   C.   10%   D.   50%

19. In which one of the following laboratories and years was the total number of tests sent   19.____
    out in the months of April, May, and June the GREATEST?
    Laboratory

     A.   X in 2003   B.   Y in 2004
     C.   Y in 2003   D.   Z in 2004

20. In 2004, the ONLY test performed in Laboratory Z to show a steady decrease was   20.____

     A.   sickle cells   B.   white blood count
     C.   hemoglobin   D.   pregnancy tests

21. The one of the following methods of training a newly employed technician which is MOST   21.____
    likely to give him experience in many laboratory functions in a relatively short period of
    time is the _____ method.

     A.   job rotation   B.   sensitivity training
     C.   role playing   D.   conference

22. If it becomes necessary for you, as a supervisor, to give a subordinate employee confi-   22.____
    dential information, the MOST effective of the following steps to take to make sure the
    information is kept confidential by the employee is to

     A.   tell the employee that the information is confidential and is not to be repeated
     B.   threaten the employee with disciplinary action if the information is repeated
     C.   offer the employee a merit increase as an incentive for keeping the information
        confidential
     D.   remind the employee at least twice a day that the information is confidential and is
        not to be repeated

23. Assume that you are a supervisor of a laboratory, and one of your subordinates brings to   23.____
    your attention the fact that another subordinate is taking home small, inexpensive items
    which are city property from the laboratory.
    The BEST of the following courses of action for you to take with regard to the accused
    employee is to

A. make no mention of your knowledge of these thefts; the items are inexpensive any-way

B. have a discussion with the employee, since these small thefts might lead to bigger ones

C. wait until you observe the employee taking something from the laboratory and *catch him in the act*

D. give a lecture to your entire group of subordinates on honesty in the laboratory

24. Assume that you are a supervisor of a laboratory, and your supervisor informs you of a serious mistake made in the analysis of an important test performed by one of your sub-ordinate technicians.
You should consider this action on the part of your supervisor as   24.____

A. *undesirable;* your supervisor should have gone straight to the technician who per-formed the test

B. *desirable;* it gives you an opportunity to talk to the employee, find out why the mis-take was made, and try to make sure there are no more serious mistakes

C. *undesirable;* your supervisor should have complained to the personnel office in your agency to make a note of the mistake in the technician's personnel file

D. *desirable;* you can then discipline the employee severely to teach him to be more careful in the future

25. Assume that you, as a supervisor of a laboratory, are asked to make a recommendation to your superior on a new technician who is about to complete his probationary period. The technician's performance, even after several conferences with him, is unsatisfactory, his work habits are poor, and he does not take his work seriously.
For you to make an UNFAVORABLE recommendation about this employee, which might result in his dismissal, would be   25.____

A. *desirable;* this action would be fair and justifiable to both the employee and the organization

B. *undesirable;* the employee passed his Civil Service test and should eventually become satisfactory

C. *desirable;* your superiors expect that a certain proportion of probationers will fail

D. *undesirable;* the employee should be given a chance to work elsewhere before an evaluation of his performance is made

———————

KEY (CORRECT ANSWERS)

1.	B		11.	A
2.	C		12.	C
3.	C		13.	C
4.	B		14.	A
5.	A		15.	B
6.	C		16.	C
7.	A		17.	C
8.	C		18.	A
9.	B		19.	A
10.	B		20.	A

21. A
22. A
23. B
24. B
25. A

———

EXAMINATION SECTION
TEST 1

DIRECTIONS: Each question or incomplete statement is followed by several suggested answers or completions. Select the one that BEST answers the question or completes the statement. *PRINT THE LETTER OF THE CORRECT ANSWER IN THE SPACE AT THE RIGHT.*

1. Which one of the following solutions has the LOWEST pH above neutrality? 1 N _____.

   1._____

     A. sodium carbonate   B. potassium hydroxide
     C. sodium bicarbonate   D. sodium hydroxide

2. Which one of the following solutions has the HIGHEST pH below neutrality? 1 N _____ acid.

   2._____

     A. hydrochloric   B. acetic
     C. sulfuric   D. nitric

3. The one of the following body fluids which normally has the LOWEST pH is

   3._____

     A. whole blood   B. cerebrospinal fluid
     C. gastric contents   D. urine

4. Which pH indicator changes from a colored to a colorless solution when the pH of a solution is decreased from 10 to 5?

   4._____

     A. Brom phenol blue   B. Methyl red
     C. Phenol red   D. Phenolphthalein

5. The mordant used when preparing a gram stain is

   5._____

     A. Gentian violet   B. alcohol
     C. iodine   D. safranin

6. Of the following, the LEAST common of the white blood cells in human blood is the

   6._____

     A. eosinophil   B. neutraphil
     C. lymphocyte   D. basophil

7. Which one of the following compounds is a carbohydrate?

   7._____

     A. Albumin   B. Adenine
     C. Cholesterol   D. Inulin

8. Which substance commonly added to blood is NOT an anticoagulant?

   8._____

     A. Sodium oxalate
     B. Heparin
     C. Ethylenediamine tetraacetate
     D. Sodium fluoride

9. Which substance is miscible with water?

   9._____

     A. Alcohol   B. Chloroform
     C. Toluene   D. Immersion oil

10. Which substance is NOT a surface-active agent?   10.____

    A. EDTA   B. Soap
    C. Desoxycholate   D. TRITON X

11. Which sugar is the same as levulose?   11.____

    A. Glucose   B. Galactose
    C. Fructose   D. Lactose

12. Biochemical reactions that proceed at rates lower than their maximum can be speeded   12.____
up by all of the following EXCEPT

    A. addition of an enzyme
    B. increasing the pH to 11.0
    C. increasing the temperature
    D. addition of more substrate

13. You are measuring the optical density of a colored solution in a spectrophotometer. You   13.____
first make a measurement using a tube with a 16-mm diameter. Then, using an adapter,
you take another measurement with the solution in a tube that has a 10-mm diameter.
The optical density reading of the second tube should be of the first tube.

    A. about two-thirds higher than that
    B. the same as that
    C. lower than that
    D. about one-third higher than that

14. Penicillin G powder has a potency of 1677 units per mg. If a vial of penicillin G contains 1   14.____
million units, how many ml of water must be added to the vial to make a solution of penicillin G containing 10,000 micrograms per ml?

    A. 10   B. 60   C. 100   D. 600

15. You are preparing the following: (1) add 28 G of disodium phosphate to 1 liter of water;   15.____
(2) add 27.6 G of monosodium phosphate to another liter of water; and (3) mix 77 ml of
solution (1) with 23 ml of solution (2). The resultant product should be a

    A. buffer solution   B. white precipitate
    C. pH indicator   D. lipid solvent

16. You have 10 ml of a solution with a specific gravity of 1.25.   16.____
In order to have an amount of distilled water that has the same weight as that solution,
you must have how many ml of the distilled water?

    A. 7.5   B. 10   C. 12.5   D. 15

17. Assume that 1 ml of a suspension of bacteria is diluted into 9 ml of saline. One ml of this   17.____
diluted suspension is again diluted into another 9 ml of saline. This procedure is
repeated two more times. Finally, 0.1 ml of the last dilution is spread onto a nutrient agar
plate, and the plate is incubated. After allowing for growth, there are 150 bacterial colo-
nies on the plate. The number of bacteria in the original suspension was

    A. 1.5×10^5 B. 1.5×10^6 C. 1.5×10^7 D. 1.5×10^{10}

18. The normal value of an adult male microhematocrit determination is   18._____

    A. 17%   B. 25%   C. 38%   D. 47%

19. How many microliters (lambdas) of a 1:250 dilution of erythrocytes must be added to 10   19._____
ml of saline to give a 1:50,000 dilution of the erythrocytes?

    A. 20   B. 50   C. 200   D. 5000

20. Assume that a urine sample was measured with a hydrometer, and the value was found   20._____
to be 1.036.
Of the following, the MOST likely explanation is that the urine sample

    A. was too diluted
    B. was taken over a 24-hour period
    C. contained too many dissolved substances
    D. contained erythrocytes

KEY (CORRECT ANSWERS)

1.	C		11.	C
2.	B		12.	B
3.	C		13.	C
4.	D		14.	B
5.	C		15.	A
6.	D		16.	C
7.	D		17.	C
8.	D		18.	D
9.	A		19.	B
10.	A		20.	C

TEST 2

DIRECTIONS: Each question or incomplete statement is followed by several suggested answers or completions. Select the one that BEST answers the question or completes the statement. *PRINT THE LETTER OF THE CORRECT ANSWER IN THE SPACE AT THE RIGHT.*

1. A 1 N solution of a compound with two replaceable hydrogens should be prepared by adding one gram molecular weight of the compound to _____ ml of solute.   1.____

   A. 100   B. 500   C. 1000   D. 2000

2. The amount of solids in 1 liter of urine may be estimated by multiplying the last two figures of the specific gravity of the urine by 2.6.   2.____
   If a given sample of urine has a specific gravity of 1.018, how many grams of solids are there in 500 ml of the solution?

   A. 9.0   B. 13.0   C. 23.4   D. 46.8

3. Thirty-seven degrees centigrade MOST closely approximates which one of the following temperatures?   3.____

   A. Temperature at which water boils
   B. Normal body temperature
   C. Normal refrigerator temperature
   D. Temperature at which water freezes

4. The procedure in which a blood smear from a finger is stained with Wright's stain, examined under a microscope, and the number of each type of leukocyte is counted is known as a   4.____

   A. GTT   B. 2 hr pp
   C. hematocrit   D. differential count

5. The term *target cell* refers to a   5.____

   A. red blood cell
   B. white blood cell
   C. heart muscle cell
   D. beta cell of the pancreas

6. The solution which should NOT be used in an emergency to extinguish a small paper fire is   6.____

   A. benzene   B. 0.1 N NaOH
   C. dilute HCl   D. phosphate buffer

7. Which one of the following parasitic diseases would be the MOST likely to cause changes in the blood?   7.____

   A. Amoebiasis   B. Tapeworm
   C. Malaria   D. Trichomonas

8. Cross-matching of blood will test for *all* of the following blood types EXCEPT type   8.____

   A. A   B. B   C.)   D. Rh

9. Hematomas may sometimes develop after collecting blood from the arm vein for *all* of the following reasons EXCEPT failure to

    9.____

    A. use a needle that is large enough
    B. have the needle completely in the vein
    C. release the tourniquet before withdrawing the needle
    D. apply finger pressure to the wound for sufficient time

10. Certain unheated sera, when mixed with incompatible blood cells, will destroy the cells. Heating the sera at 56° C for 30 minutes prevents this reaction.
This cellular destruction is called

    10.____

    A. isoagglutination   B. Rh hemolysis
    C. isohemolysis   D. false agglutination

11. The anti-sera used for testing blood groupings must agglutinate Type A cells in a dilution of AT LEAST

    11.____

    A. 1:10   B. 1:100   C. 1:128   D. 1:512

12. Which blood typing system does NOT test for the Rh factor?

    12.____

    A. Wiener   B. Lewis
    C. Fisher-Race   D. Rosenfield

13. A phenylhydrazine test is used to identify which one of the following types of compounds?

    13.____

    A. Sugars   B. Hormones
    C. Blood gases   D. Urinary salts

14. Which procedure is essential for the determination of acid phosphatase, but is NOT used to determine alkaline phosphatase?

    14.____

    A. Incubating the reaction mixture at a temperature of 37° C
    B. Using a spectrophotometer
    C. Adding merthiolate for sterility
    D. Keeping the specimen cold at all times

15. Which sugar that might be found in the urine does NOT give a positive Benedict's or Clinitest reaction?

    15.____

    A. Sucrose   B. Fructose   C. Ribose   D. Galactose

16. Which one of the following findings in a 24-hour urine sample would be considered ABNORMAL?

    16.____

    A. Glucose
    B. pH - 6.2
    C. Specific gravity - 1.021
    D. Volume - 2700 ml

17. How should a protein-free filtrate of blood be prepared? By   17._____

    A.   using only whole blood
    B.   adding acid to serum
    C.   allowing the blood to clot
    D.   inactivating prothrombin

18. When you collect blood by use of the finger-puncture method, you should discard the first   18._____
drop of blood because it

    A.   is contaminated with skin bacteria
    B.   is diluted with tissue matter and fluid
    C.   has a higher white cell count
    D.   is diluted with skin moisture

19. A blood smear from a finger stained with Wright's stain shows erythrocytes in *stacked*   19._____
chips arrangement.
This cell arrangement is called

    A.   agglutination   B.   rouleaux formation
    C.   Hargrave's cells   D.   hyaline casts

20. When a tube of heparinized blood is centrifuged, a layer of white blood cells forms above   20._____
the erythrocytes. This reaction occurs because

    A.   white cells are motile and red cells are not
    B.   white cells are heavier than red cells
    C.   red cells are larger than white cells
    D.   red cells are heavier than white cells

KEY (CORRECT ANSWERS)

1.	B	11.	C
2.	C	12.	B
3.	B	13.	A
4.	D	14.	D
5.	A	15.	A
6.	A	16.	D
7.	C	17.	B
8.	D	18.	B
9.	A	19.	B
10.	C	20.	D

EXAMINATION SECTION
TEST 1

DIRECTIONS: Each question or incomplete statement is followed by several suggested answers or completions. Select the one that BEST answers the question or completes the statement. *PRINT THE LETTER OF THE CORRECT ANSWER IN THE SPACE AT THE RIGHT.*

1. The part of the compound microscope on which the slide is placed is called the   1.____

    A. base   B. condenser   C. diaphragm   D. stage

2. The part of an analytical balance which supports the arms is called the   2.____

    A. beam   B. pointer
    C. rest point   D. spirit level

3. Hematocrit can be determined by packing the red cells in a blood sample with a(n)   3.____

    A. centrifuge   B. condenser
    C. extractor   D. pipetting machine

4. The instrument used for measuring the pressure of liquids or gases is known as a   4.____

    A. calorimeter   B. colorimeter
    C. manometer   D. micrometer

5. Specific gravity can be measured with the   5.____

    A. homogenizer   B. hydrometer
    C. hygrometer   D. turbidometer

6. Steam under pressure is sometimes used to sterilize laboratory equipment. The apparatus used for this is called a(n)   6.____

    A. hot air oven   B. pyrometer
    C. Arnold sterilizer   D. autoclave

7. When using an analytical balance, the balance case should be closed while final adjustments are made.
This is done to prevent errors from   7.____

    A. air currents   B. dust
    C. humidity   D. static electricity

8. The one of the following pieces of laboratory equipment which is subject to *strike back* is the   8.____

    A. analytical balance   B. Berkefeld filter
    C. bunsen burner   D. simple microscope

9. For ordinary laboratory purposes, the FINAL step in cleaning glassware should be a rinse in   9.____

    A. chromic acid   B. distilled water
    C. ethyl alcohol   D. trisodium phosphate

10. The one of the following that is GENERALLY sterilized with a flame is a   10._____

    A. filter   B. pipette   C. slide   D. test tube

11. A microtome is GENERALLY used to   11._____

    A. distill water   B. record sounds
    C. section tissue   D. weigh small objects

12. When labels are placed on glass slides, the labels can be protected by painting with   12._____

    A. ethylene glycol   B. glycerol
    C. melted paraffin   D. petroleum ether

13. All of the following oils may be used with an oil-immersion objective EXCEPT _____ oil.   13._____

    A. cedarwood   B. immersion   C. machine   D. mineral

14. The purpose of the coarse adjuster of a compound microscope is to   14._____

    A. adjust the intensity of the light
    B. move the stage so that the area to be examined is beneath the objective
    C. obtain approximate focus
    D. obtain exact focus

15. The magnification of any combination of objectives and oculars may be obtained by _____ the magnification of the   15._____

    A. adding; ocular   B. multiplying; ocular
    C. subtracting; ocular   D. subtracting; objective

16. The purpose of the mirror on a compound microscope is to   16._____

    A. direct light downward through the ocular
    B. direct light upward through the condenser
    C. reflect light away from the stage
    D. reflect the image onto a screen

17. In some laboratories, file folders borrowed by technicians from other laboratories are returned to a central location to be refiled by a technician from that laboratory. This practice is   17._____

    A. *desirable;* to prevent misfiling, only technicians who know the filing system should refile material
    B. *undesirable;* this creates extra work for laboratory personnel
    C. *desirable;* technicians from other laboratories might come across confidential information in the files
    D. *undesirable;* folders should be returned to the files immediately in case others want to use them

18. If small documents must be filed in standard size file folders, the BEST way to prevent them from becoming lost or damaged is to   18._____

    A. fasten them to the cover of the folder
    B. glue them to standard-size paper
    C. place them neatly in the back of the folder
    D. staple them together and place them in the front of the folder

19. 1,000,000 may be represented as

    A. 10^3 B. 10^5 C. 10^6 D. 10^{10}

20. 35° Centigrade equals

    A. 70° F   B. 95° F   C. 100° F   D. 120° F

21. $10^3 \times 10^4$ equals

    A. 10^7 B. 10^{12} C. 100^7 D. 100^{12}

22. If a mixture is made up of one part Substance A, 3 parts Substance B, and 12 parts Substance C, the proportion of Substance A in the mixture is

    A. 4%   B. 6 1/4%   C. 16%   D. 62 1/2%

23. If 5 grams of a chemical are enough to perform a certain laboratory test 9 times, the quantity of the chemical needed to perform this test 1,350 times would be _____ grams.

    A. 30   B. 150   C. 270   D. 750

24. If it takes 7 grams of a certain substance to make 5 liters of a solution, the quantity of the substance needed to make 4 liters of the solution is _____ grams.

    A. 2.85   B. 4.70   C. 5.60   D. 8.75

25. If it takes 3 grams of Substance A and 7 grams of Substance B to make 4 liters of a solution, how many grams of Substances A and B does it take to make 5 liters of the solution?

    _____ of Substance A and of Substance B.

    A. 3.35; 6.65   B. 3.50; 7.50
    C. 3.75; 8.75   D. 4; 7

26. A certain type of laboratory test can be performed by a laboratory technician in 20 minutes.
Three laboratory technicians can perform 243 such tests in _____ hours.

    A. 16   B. 20   C. 27   D. 81

27. Pairs of shatterproof plastic safety glasses cost $3.80 each, but an 8% discount is given on orders of six pairs or more. Pairs of straight blade dissecting scissors cost $14.40 a dozen with a 12% discount on orders of two dozen or more.
The total cost of eight pairs of safety glasses and 30 pairs of dissecting scissors is MOST NEARLY

    A. $59.65   B. $62.10   C. $66.40   D. $73.15

28. On July 1, your laboratory has 280 usable 20-gauge needles on hand. On August 1, 15% of these needles have been lost or damaged beyond repair. On August 15, a new shipment of 50 needles is received by the laboratory, but 10% of these arrive damaged and are returned to the seller.
At this point, the number of usable 20-gauge needles on hand would be

    A. 238   B. 283   C. 288   D. 325

29. A certain laboratory procedure can be completed by a laboratory technician in 15 minutes.
    If your lab is assigned 30 such tests, and they must be completed within 3 hours, the MINIMUM number of technicians that would have to be assigned to this task is

    A. 2   B. 3   C. 4   D. 5   29._____

30. An endothermic reaction is one in which   30._____

    A. the boiling point is raised
    B. the boiling point is lowered
    C. heat is liberated
    D. heat is absorbed

31. A substance which increases the rate of a chemical reaction is termed a(n)   31._____

    A. isotope   B. polymer   C. catalyst   D. hydrate

32. The process of converting a solid into a liquid by means of heat is called   32._____

    A. incineration   B. fusion
    C. distillation   D. carbonization

33. The valence of the nitrate (NO_3) radical is   33._____

    A. 0   B. -1   C. -2   D. -3

34. The chemical name for wood alcohol is   34._____

    A. methanol   B. ethanol
    C. butanol   D. absolute alcohol

35. The molecular weight of hydrogen is MOST NEARLY   35._____

    A. 1   B. 2   C. 14   D. 16

36. In a laboratory filtration, the solid left on the filter paper is USUALLY called the   36._____

    A. distillate   B. filtrate
    C. precipitate   D. solute

Questions 37-40.

DIRECTIONS: Questions 37 through 40 pertain to the meaning of terms which may be encountered in laboratory work. For each question, select the option whose meaning is MOST NEARLY the same as that of the numbered item.

37. atrophied   37._____

    A. enlarged   B. relaxed
    C. strengthened   D. wasted

38. leucocyte   38._____

    A. white cell   B. red cell
    C. epithelial cell   D. dermal cell

20

39. permeable

    A. volatile   B. variable
    C. flexible   D. penetrable

39.____

40. attenuate

    A. dilute   B. infect
    C. oxidize   D. strengthen

40.____

KEY (CORRECT ANSWERS)

1. D	11. C	21. A	31. C
2. A	12. C	22. B	32. B
3. A	13. C	23. D	33. B
4. C	14. C	24. C	34. A
5. B	15. B	25. C	35. B
6. D	16. B	26. C	36. C
7. A	17. A	27. A	37. D
8. C	18. B	28. B	38. A
9. B	19. C	29. B	39. D
10. C	20. B	30. D	40. A

TEST 2

DIRECTIONS: Each question or incomplete statement is followed by several suggested answers or completions. Select the one that BEST answers the question or completes the statement. *PRINT THE LETTER OF THE CORRECT ANSWER IN THE SPACE AT THE RIGHT.*

1. Assume that there are six laboratory technicians working in a certain laboratory. Four of them are well-trained, efficient workers and can perform a certain procedure in 15 minutes. The other two are newly-hired and have not completed their training. It takes each of them twice as long to perform that procedure.
   If all six are assigned to perform 70 such procedures, they can complete the work in _____ hours.

   A. 3   B. 3 1/2   C. 4   D. 4 1/2   1.____

2. Inoculation under the skin is termed   2.____

   A. subdural   B. subcutaneous
   C. per os   D. sublingual

3. The four major blood groups are GENERALLY designated as groups   3.____

   A. A, B, AB, O   B. A, B, C, Rh
   C. A, B, K, O   D. AB, K, Rh, O

4. In acid-fast staining, the acid-fast bacteria are stained   4.____

   A. red   B. green   C. brown   D. blue

5. The optimum temperature for the growth of most pathogenic bacteria is APPROXIMATELY   5.____

   A. 35 °C   B. 55 °C   C. 75 °C   D. 95 °C

6. You are about to draw blood from a patient who speaks with a heavy foreign accent. He becomes very upset and, speaking rapidly, tries to explain something to you. However, you cannot understand him.
   The BEST thing for you to do would be to   6.____

   A. ask the person to speak slowly and have him repeat what he is trying to communicate
   B. draw the blood but note on the lab request that the patient became upset
   C. explain to the patient that the test will not hurt him and then draw the blood
   D. omit the blood test since it is upsetting the patient

7. The number of red blood corpuscles in each cubic millimeter of normal adult human blood is within the range of   7.____

   A. 75,000 to 85,000   B. 600,000 to 800,000
   C. 4,000,000 to 6,000,000   D. 10,000,000 to 20,000,000

8. The presence of casts is determined in the microscopic examination of   8.____

   A. spinal fluid   B. blood
   C. urine   D. feces

9. Benedict's reagent is used in urine analysis to test for   9.____

    A. ammonia   B. bile   C. protein   D. sugar

10. Bacteria GENERALLY reproduce by   10.____

    A. fusion   B. spore formation
    C. conjugation   D. binary fission

11. Ringworm is a disease caused by   11.____

    A. worms   B. viruses   C. molds   D. bacteria

12. Bacteria which grow best in the presence of free oxygen are called   12.____

    A. thermophiles   B. mesophiles
    C. anaerobes   D. aerobes

13. Of the following organisms, those GENERALLY considered to be the smallest in size are the   13.____

    A. viruses   B. rickettsiae
    C. molds   D. bacteria

14. The Ziehl-Neelsen staining method is GENERALLY associated with the _____ stain.   14.____

    A. spore   B. Gram   C. capsule   D. acid-fast

15. The acid-fast stain is GENERALLY associated with the diagnosis of   15.____

    A. diphtheria   B. syphilis
    C. tuberculosis   D. typhoid fever

16. The Schick test is used to determine susceptibility to   16.____

    A. typhoid fever   B. tetanus
    C. pneumonia   D. diphtheria

17. In the Gram method, the Gram positive bacteria are stained   17.____

    A. brown   B. green   C. violet   D. yellow

18. The RECOMMENDED method for storing metallic sodium is   18.____

    A. in alcohol
    B. in a box in the refrigerator
    C. under kerosene
    D. under water

19. The BEST way to put out a chemical fire is to   19.____

    A. smother it with a cylinder of nitrogen
    B. flood it with water
    C. use a carbon dioxide fire extinguisher
    D. use a carbon tetrachloride fire extinguisher

20. The one of the following chemicals which is very flammable and should NOT be exposed   20.____
    to any flames or sparks is

    A. carbon disulfide   B. formaldehyde
    C. methylene chloride   D. potassium iodide

21. Which of the following solutions should NOT be kept in an ordinary refrigerator?   21.____
    A(n) _____ solution of _____ .

    A. alcohol; gram stain   B. chloroform; cholesterol
    C. water; ammonium nitrate   D. ether; triglycerides

22. The process whereby crystals lose their water of crystallization on exposure to the atmo-   22.____
    sphere is termed

    A. sublimation   B. efflorescence
    C. declination   D. decantation

23. A substance used to increase the stability of a dispersion of one liquid in another is   23.____
    called a(n)

    A. buffer   B. catalyst   C. aerator   D. emulsifier

24. The RECOMMENDED method of disposing of volatile, flammable solvents is to   24.____

    A. burn them in a secluded place
    B. evaporate them on a steam bath in a hood
    C. pour them down the sink with a lot of water
    D. put them in a steel garbage can with a tight-fitting lid

Questions 25-34.

DIRECTIONS: The following is a list of patients who were referred by various clinics to the
laboratory for tests. After each name is a patient identification number. Questions 25 through 34 are to be answered on the basis of the information contained in this list and the explanation accompanying it.

The first digit refers to the clinic which made the referral:

    1 - Cardiac   6 - Hematology
    2 - Renal   7 - Gynecology
    3 - Pediatrics   8 - Neurology
    4 - Opthalmology   9 - Gastroenterology
    5 - Orthopedics

The second digit refers to the sex of the patient:
    1 - male   2 - female

The third and fourth digits give the age of the patient.

The last two digits give the day of the month the laboratory tests were performed.

LABORATORY REFERRALS DURING JANUARY

Adams, Jacqueline	320917	Miller, Michael	111806
Black, Leslie	813406	Pratt, William	214411
Cook, Marie	511616	Rogers, Ellen	722428
Fisher, Pat	914625	Saunders, Sally	310229
Jackson , Lee	923212	Wilson, Jan	416715
James, Linda	624621	Wyatt, Mark	321326
Lane, Arthur	115702		

25. According to the list, the number of women referred to the laboratory during January was   25.____

    A. 4   B. 5   C. 6   D. 7

26. The clinic from which the MOST patients were referred was   26.____

    A. Cardiac   B. Gynecology   C. Opthamology   D. Pediatrics

27. The YOUNGEST patient referred from any clinic other than Pediatrics was   27.____

    A. Leslie Black   B. Marie Cook
    C. Arthur Lane   D. Sally Saunders

28. The number of patients whose laboratory tests were performed on or before January 21 was   28.____

    A. 7   B. 8   C. 9   D. 10

29. The number of patients referred for laboratory tests who are under age 45 is   29.____

    A. 7   B. 8   C. 9   D. 10

30. The OLDEST patient referred to the clinic during January was   30.____

    A. Jacqueline Adams   B. Linda James
    C. Arthur Lane   D. Jan Wilson

31. The ONLY patient treated in the Orthopedics clinic was   31.____

    A. Marie Cook   B. Pat Fisher
    C. Ellen Rogers   D. Jan Wilson

32. A woman age 37 was referred from the Hematology clinic to the laboratory. Her laboratory tests were performed on January 9.
Her identification number would be   32.____

    A. 610937   B. 623709   C. 613790   D. 623790

33. A man was referred for lab tests from the Orthopedics clinic. He is 30 years old, and his tests were performed on January 6.
His identification number would be   33.____

    A. 413006   B. 510360   C. 513006   D. 613060

34. A 4-year-old boy was referred from Pediatrics clinic to 34. _____ have laboratory tests on January 23. His identification number was

    A. 310422   B. 310423   C. 310433   D. 320403

                                                   34._____

Questions 35-38.

DIRECTIONS: Questions 35 through 38 are to be answered SOLELY on the basis of the information contained in the following table.

DEATH RATE FROM PULMONARY TUBERCULOSIS ACCORDING TO OCCUPATION (per 100,000 population) (County X, 1990)	
Unskilled workers.....................................	185
Semiskilled workers.................................	102
Skilled workers and foremen....................	72
Clerks	66
Agricultural workers................................	47
Managers..	43
Professionals	26

35. The occupation whose death rate was about one-fourth the death rate for semiskilled workers is

    A. agricultural workers   B. clerks
    C. managers   D. professionals

35._____

36. If 18% of the agricultural workers who died from pulmonary tuberculosis were women, out of 100,000 agricultural workers, the number of women who died from pulmonary tuberculosis is

    A. 3   B. 9   C. 18   D. 29

36._____

37. If there were 3,400,000 managers in County X in 1990, the number who died from pulmonary tuberculosis was

    A. 146   B. 1,151   C. 1,462   D. 1,849

37._____

38. Among the skilled workers and foremen who died from pulmonary tuberculosis in 1990, one-quarter had the expenses of their illness paid for entirely by insurance, and one-third had part of their medical expenses paid for by insurance.
Out of 100,000 skilled workers and foremen, the number who had all or part of their medical expenses paid for by insurance was MOST NEARLY

    A. 18   B. 24   C. 37   D. 42

38._____

39. Assume that one of your subordinates asks you for advice on a personal problem. The BEST thing for you to do would be to

    A. explain to the worker that personal problems should not be discussed during working hours
    B. have the worker transferred to a simple job where his preoccupation with his problem will not cause serious errors
    C. listen sympathetically to his story without telling him what to do about the problem
    D. tell the worker you will think over his problem and advise him the following day

39._____

26

40. Accuracy is extremely important in most laboratory work. If you find that a member of   40.____
your staff has made several errors in the past few weeks, the BEST thing for you to do
would be to

    A. ask him why he is being so careless
    B. discuss his inadequate performance at a meeting of your staff to see if they can
        suggest ways he can improve
    C. explain to him in private where his work in inaccurate and how he can improve it in
        the future
    D. threaten to give him a poor evaluation unless his work improves

-----

KEY (CORRECT ANSWERS)

1.	B	11.	C	21.	D	31.	A
2.	B	12.	D	22.	B	32.	B
3.	A	13.	A	23.	D	33.	C
4.	A	14.	D	24.	B	34.	B
5.	A	15.	C	25.	B	35.	D
6.	A	16.	D	26.	D	36.	B
7.	C	17.	C	27.	B	37.	C
8.	C	18.	C	28.	C	38.	D
9.	D	19.	C	29.	C	39.	C
10.	D	20.	A	30.	D	40.	C

EXAMINATION SECTION
TEST 1

DIRECTIONS: Each question or incomplete statement is followed by several suggested
answers or completions. Select the one that *BEST* answers the question or
completes the statement. *PRINT THE LETTER OF THE CORRECT ANSWER
IN THE SPACE AT THE RIGHT.*

1. The one of the following which is the *MOST* effective disinfectant for laboratory equip-   1.____
ment is

    A.   ethanol   B.   phenol   C.   zephiran   D.   mercurochrome

2. Of the following, the *MAJOR* reason why mouth, pipetting has generally been replaced   2.____
by other methods is that

    A.   mouth pipetting increases the risk of infection
    B.   other methods allow greater accuracy than mouth pipetting
    C.   mouth pipetting techniques are difficult for new technicians to learn
    D.   other methods are less expensive

3. A fire breaks out because of a short circuit in some electrical laboratory equipment. Of   3.____
the following, the type of fire extinguisher which is *BEST to* use on this type of fire is the

    A.   soda-acid type   B.   gas cartridge water type
    C.   carbon dioxide type   D.   foam type

4. Of the following, the *BEST* first-aid treatment for a technician who has spilled acid on his   4.____
hands is the *immediate* application of

    A.   large quantities of running water
    B.   feandages soaked in cold water
    C.   vaseline or other unguents
    D.   mild vinegar solution

5. Of the following, the *BEST* first-aid treatment for a technician who suffers a first degree   5.____
burn on his finger is the *immediate* application of

    A.   any mild acid solution   B.   plain cool water
    C.   clean oil or grease   D.   a white cloth bandage

6. The *MAXIMUM* magnification of the light microscope is approximately   6.____

    A.   1000 X   B.   5000 X   C.   10,000 X   D.   100,000 X

7. The one of the following which will weaken an acid the *MOST* is diluting it *with*   7.____

    A. HNO_3 B. H_2O C.   HCl   D. H_2SO_4

8. For safety, volatile solutions of ether or chloroform are *BEST* stored   8.____

    A.   at floor level   B.   in explosion-proof refrigerators
    C.   under water   D.   in pressurized lockers

9. Of the following, an overhead safety shower is *MOST* likely to be found in a laboratory which routinely uses   9.____

   A. highly dilute solutions   B. dry sodium chloride
   C. large quantities of hydrochloric acid   D. fume hoods

10. One micron equals *what* part of a millimeter?   10.____

   A. 1/1000th   B. 1/10,000th   C. 1/100,000th   D. 1/1,000,000th

11. Of the following, the *FIRST* step th.at should be taken when cutting a piece of glass tub-   11.____
    ing into smaller sections is to

   A. scratch the glass tubing by passing a hard-steel knife once across the glass
   B. scratch the glass tubing by passing a hard-steel knife back and forth over the glass tubing
   C. heat the glass tubing over a Bunsen burner at the spot where the glass tubing is to be cut
   D. strike the glass tubing against a hard surface at the spot where the cut is to be made

12. In using a microscope, the maximum magnification achieved by using a 10 X eyepiece   12.____
    and a high dry objective is, most nearly,

   A. 100 X   B. 320 X   C. 450 X   D. 776 X

Questions 13-20.

DIRECTIONS: Questions 13 through 20 are to be answered *SOLELY* on the basis of the TEST REPORT FORM, TEST PROCEDURES, EQUIVALENCY TABLES, and PATIENT DATA given below.

TEST REPORT FORM

Kellman Differential		Rosewald Value	
Phase I	Phase II	Type I	Type II
☐ a. High	☐ a. High		
☐ b. Normal	☐ b. Normal		
☐ c. Low	☐ c. Low		
☐ d. Indeterminate	☐ d. Indeterminate		

TEST PROCEDURES

RAW TEST RESULTS: Four different *raw test results* may be obtained for each patient:

   a. Kellman Differential Phase I result (= P_I)
   b. Kellman Differential Phase II result C= P_{II})
   c. Rosewald Type I result (= T_I)
   d. Rosewald Type II result (= T_{II})

KELLMAN DIFFERENTIAL: The P_I and P_{II} are obtained for each patient and compared against the appropriate tables under the heading EQUIVALENCY TABLES. Each result is reported by checking off the corresponding box (High, Normal, Low, or Indeterminate) in the appropriate space on the TEST REPORT FORM.

ROSEWALD VALUE: The Type I Rosewald *Value* is computed and reported *only* for patients whose P_I is either *Low* or *indeterminate*. This value is computed as $T_I - P_I$. It is reported by entering the resulting number in the appropriate box on the TEST REPORT FORM.

The Type II Rosewald value is computed and reported *only* for patients whose P_{II} is either *Low* or *indeterminate*. This value is computed as $T_{II} - P_{II}$ It is reported by entering the resulting number in the appropriate box on the TEST REPORT FORM.

EQUIVALENCY TABLES

Report Category	Kellman Differential							
	Phase I (P_I)				Phase II (P_{II})			
	Males		Females		Males		Females	
	Under Age 40	Over Age 40	Under Age 40	Over Age 40	Under Age 40	Over Age 40	Under Age 40	Over Age 40
High	Over 15	Over 10	Over 20	Over 17	Over 25	Over 20	Over 35	Over 30
Normal	10 to 15	7 to 10	15 to 20	10 to 17	17 to 25	14 to 20	25 to 35	20 to 30
Low	6 to 9	4 to 6	9 to 14	6 to 9	8 to 16	7 to 13	11 to 24	9 to 19
Indeterminate	Under 6	Under 4	Under 9	Under 6	Under 8	Under 7	Under 11	Under 9

PATIENT DATA

Patient Number	Name	Age	P_I	P_{II}
#1003	Mr. Francis Dole	25	10	14
#3627	Mrs. Leslie Smith	50	5	14
#5627	Mr. Ling Chou	62	8	14
#0001	Miss B. Merchant	17	14	40

13. The *one* of the following patients whose Kellman Differential Phase II would be reported as "High" is   13.____

   A. #1003   B. #3627   C. #5627   D. #0001

14. The *one* of the following which would *NOT* be reported as "Normal" is the Kellman Differential Phase   14.____

   A. I for Patient #1003   B. I for Patient #5627
   C. II for Patient #1003   D. II for Patient #5627

15. The box under "Phase I" which, should be checked off on the TEST REPORT FORM for Patient #3627 is   15.____

   A. a   B. b   C. c   D. d

16. The Kellman Differential Phase II which should be reported for Mrs. Leslie Smith is   16.___

    A. High   B. Normal   C. Low   D. Indeterminate

17. The number of patients for whom it would be necessary to report the Type I Rosewald   17.___
    Value is

    A. 1   B. 2   C. 3   D. 4

18. The *one* of the following patients for whom it would be necessary to report *BOTH* the   18.___
    Type I Rosewald Value *AND* the Type II Rosewald Value is

    A. Leslie Smith   B. Francis Dole
    C. Ling Chou   D. B. Merchant

19. If T_I equals 50 for each patient for whom the Type I Rosewald value must be reported, the   19.___
    patient whose reported Type I Rosewald value would be numerically *LARGEST* is

    A. #1003   B. #3627   C. #5627   D. #0001

20. If T_{II} equals 100 for each patient for whom the Type II Rosewald Value must be reported,   20.___
    the *two* patients whose reported Type II Rosewald Values will be *numerically equal* are

    A. Francis Dole and Ling Chou
    B. Leslie Smith and B. Merchant
    C. Francis Dole and Leslie Smith
    D. Ling Chou and B. Merchant

———

KEY (CORRECT ANSWERS)

1.	B		11.	A
2.	A		12.	C
3.	C		13.	D
4.	A		14.	C
5.	B		15.	D
6.	A		16.	C
7.	B		17.	B
8.	B		18.	A
9.	C		19.	B
10.	A		20.	C

———

TEST 2

DIRECTIONS: Each question or incomplete statement is, followed by several suggested answers or completions, Select the one that *BEST* answers the question or completes the statement. *PRINT THE LETTER OF THE CORRECT ANSWER IN THE SPACE AT THE RIGHT.*

Questions 1-4.

DIRECTIONS: In answering Questions 1 through 4, assume that you are a Senior Laboratory Technician responsible for maintaining the inventory and stock.

1. The following quantities of disposable syringes were used during the first six weeks of the year: 840, 756, 772, 794, 723, 789.
   If the cost of a disposable syringe is seven cents, the average *weekly cost* for disposable syringes is, most nearly,

   A. $55   B. $78   C. $85   D. $327

   1.____

2. Four pieces of glass tubing measuring 4 feet 3 inches, 6 feet 8 inches, 7 feet 2 inches, and 7 feet 6 inches are to be cut into 5-inch pieces.
   The *total number* of 5-inch pieces that can be cut from the four pieces is

   A. 60   B. 61   C. 62   D. 63

   2.____

3. Assume that a 55-gallon drum of disinfectant is to be distributed equally among eight work stations.
   The *amount* of disinfectant that each work station should receive is

   A. 7.5 gallons   B. 27.5 pints
   C. 55 pints   D. 55 quarts

   3.____

4. On June 30, an inventory indicated that there were 13 dozen petri dishes in the stockroom. During the next four weeks in July, the following quantities of petri dishes were given out by the stockroom: 23, 56, 37, 31. On August 1 no petri dishes were given out, but 9 dozens were delivered to the stockroom.
   The number of petri dishes in the stockroom *after* delivery on August 1 is

   A. 18   B. 108   C. 110   D. 117

   4.____

5. Which of the following practices is the *CORRECT* one for the laboratory technician to follow when he sets up a demonstration in the preparation room?

   A. He need not concern himself with safety factors since the demonstration is some one else's responsibility
   B. He should turn over to a responsible helper the testing of the apparatus to see that everything is safe and in working order
   C. He should realize that his responsibility ends when the set-up is moved out of the preparation room into the demonstration room
   D. He is responsible for checking all safety factors which may be involved, so that the demonstrator receives a set-up which will operate safely

   5.____

6. In the experiment in which oxygen is prepared by heating MnO_2 with $KClO_3$, serious consequences may result *if*

    A. charcoal is substituted for MnO_2
    B. charcoal is substituted for $KClO_3$
    C. KCl is substituted for $KClO_3$
    D. KCl is substituted for MnO_2

6.____

7. Solutions of mercury compounds should not be poured *directly* down the drain because they

    A. are explosive
    C. are inflammable
    B. may damage the drain pipes
    D. are heavy and will clog the drains

7.____

8. To close a bottle containing dry ice, it is *DESIRABLE* to

    A. plug it loosely with cotton
    C. plug it with a rubber stopper
    B. use a tight cork
    D. put in a ground-glass stopper

8.____

9. Which one of the following is the *BEST* place to store acids? A(n)

    A. albarene closet
    C. safe with a good combination lock
    B. metal, fire-proof cabinet
    D. special wooden acid closet

9.____

10. If a laboratory technician discovers that a pipe in the preparation room has a jagged edge, he should

    A. assign a helper to correct it
    B. correct it himself
    C. notify the demonstrator of this condition
    D. send a note to his supervisor notifying him of this condition

10.____

11. A lancet used to obtain blood should be

    A. sterilized after each use by heating in an open flame
    B. sterilized after each use by autoclaving
    C. cleaned with alcohol before and after use
    D. used only once and thrown away

11.____

12. Of the following precautions to be undertaken when ether is being used in the laboratory, the *MOST* essential is to be sure that

    A. there are no plants nearby
    C. there is no open flame in the room
    B. the windows are open
    D. none of the helpers is allergic to ether

12.____

Questions 13-20.

DIRECTIONS: In answering Questions 13 through 20, assume that you are a Senior Laboratory Technician assigned to supervise and train one or more Laboratory Technicians.

13. Of the following, a Senior Laboratory Technician assigned to supervise a group of Laboratory Technicians is *MOST* likely to help increase the work performance and satisfaction of the group if he

    A. checks their work closely and often
    B. relies heavily on strict discipline to enforce rules
    C. treats each of them in exactly the same way
    D. defends them when they are criticized unjustly

13.____

14. An increase in the workload has required a change in the work-flow procedures. In order to reduce the resistance of the Laboratory Technicians assigned to you to the changes, it would be *BEST* to

    A. give each Laboratory Technician a copy of the changes on the day the changes are to be implemented
    B. discuss the changes with the Laboratory Technicians before they are implemented
    C. convince the Laboratory Technicians that Management has ordered these changes and everybody has to comply
    D. tell the Laboratory Technicians that the current methods are not working

14.____

15. You wish to criticize a Laboratory Technician whose work, you feel, has been unnecessarily careless. Of the following, your criticism is *MOST* likely to help the technician improve his performance if you

    A. show him how his carelessness grows out of weaknesses in his personality
    B. makesure you criticize him in the company of other technicians
    C. tell him that his carelessness will probably cause a patient's death some day
    D. accompany your criticism with constructive ways he can improve his work

15.____

16. As a Senior Laboratory Technician, assume that you have been assigned the task of setting productivity standards for the Laboratory Technicians assigned to you. If you were to ask the Laboratory Technicians for their ideas on productivity standards, It would be considered

    A. *inappropriate,* because decisions of this type should be set by the supervisor without the aid of his subordinates
    B. *inappropriate,* because studies have indicated that subordinates set very low standards
    C. *appropriate,* because standards reached with the aid of subordinates are more likely to be adhered to by them
    D. appropriate, because supervisors do not really know what standards to set

16.____

17. You are concerned because the Laboratory Technicians assigned to you frequently spread false rumors they hear about changes in hospital policy. Of the following, you are *MOST* likely to help reduce the spread of these rumors if you

    A. give the Laboratory Technicians only as much information as they need to do their jobs
    B. make no comment on the rumors and allow them to run their course
    C. deliberately spread false rumors in order to embarrass those Laboratory Technicians who repeat them
    D. discredit the rumors by telling the Laboratory Technicians the facts behind the rumors

17.____

18. Assume that you, a Senior Laboratory Technician, had to separate two Laboratory Tech- 18.____
nicians assigned to you in order to stop them from fighting. You then interviewed the Laboratory Technician you considered to be the more reliable of the two in order to
determine what had happened. Your action in attempting to determine what had
occurred between the two Laboratory Technicians would generally be considered

    A. *appropriate,* because the more dependable Laboratory Technician was interviewed
    B. appropriate, because interviewing both Laboratory Technicians would result in
conflicting stories
    C. *inappropriate,* because a witness to the incident should have been interviewed
rather than one of the involved Laboratory Technicians
    D. *inappropriate,* because both Laboratory Technicians should have been interviewed

19. As a Senior Laboratory Technician, you have been assigned to supervise a Laboratory 19.____
Technician who, although capable, shows little interest in his work. Of the following, you
are *LEAST* likely to help motivate this Laboratory Technician if you

    A. relieve him of responsibility by making his decisions for him
    B. ask him for advice on how laboratory procedures could be improved
    C. encourage him to share his knowledge with trainees
    D. give him special assignments for which he is unusually qualified

20. Assume that you, a Senior Laboratory Technician, are interviewing a Laboratory Techni- 20.____
cian assigned to you whose productivity is adequate but had been much higher than
average. Which one of the following actions is most likely to result in getting the coopera-
tion of the Laboratory Technician to increase his productivity?

    A. Tell the Laboratory Technician you expect his productivity to increase because he
has worked harder in the past
    B. Let the Laboratory Technician know that you will do whatever you can for him if he
increases his productivity
    C. Set up a schedule for the Laboratory Technician and tell him that this will increase
his productivity
    D. Try to get the Laboratory Technician to suggest ways by which his productivity can
be increased and see whether he will give it a try

————

KEY (CORRECT ANSWERS)

1.	A		11.	D
2.	B		12.	C
3.	C		13.	D
4.	D		14.	B
5.	D		15.	D
6.	A		16.	C
7.	B		17.	D
8.	A		18.	D
9.	A		19.	A
10.	C		20.	D

EXAMINATION SECTION
TEST 1

DIRECTIONS: Each question or incomplete statement is followed by several suggested answers or completions. Select the one that BEST answers the question or completes the statement. *PRINT THE LETTER OF THE CORRECT ANSWER IN THE SPACE AT THE RIGHT.*

1. The equivalent weight of $CaCl_2$ (M.W. = 110) is

    A. 37   B. 55.5   C. 110   D. 220   1.____

2. 40.8 gm of mercury is used for the calibration of a pipette (Density = 13.6). What is the volume?   2.____

    A. 1   B. 2   C. 3   D. 4

3. In gas-liquid chromatography, it is necessary for the sample to be   3.____

    A. precipitated   B. pulverized
    C. soluble in water   D. volatilized

4. In flame photometry, the color of sodium in the flame is   4.____

    A. green   B. purple   C. red   D. yellow

5. Thin layer chromatography has a distinct ADVANTAGE over paper chromatography in that it   5.____

    A. can be used with aqueous solutions
    B. is cheaper
    C. is faster
    D. uses less sample

6. Of the following, the one that the halogen ions do NOT include is   6.____

    A. chloride   B. fluoride   C. iodide   D. sulfide

7. Beer's Law relates to   7.____

    A. calorimetry   B. colorimetry
    C. gas volumes   D. oxidation-reduction

8. The sulfides of lead and mercury are   8.____

    A. colloidal   B. insoluble
    C. red in color   D. soluble

9. The inert gases include all EXCEPT   9.____

    A. argon   B. krypton   C. methane   D. neon

10. Of the following metals, the one which is in a different group from the others in the periodic table is   10.____

    A. lithium   B. sodium   C. magnesium   D. cesium

11. The reaction of equimolar concentrations of NaOH and HCl is 11.____

   A. amphoteric titration   B. coulemetric titration
   C. neutralization   D. oxidation-reduction

12. 10.0 ml of a 0.1 normal solution contains 12.____

   A. 1 equivalent   B. 1 microequivalent
   C. 1 milliequivalent   D. 1 milligram

13. The assay of a compound that has maximum absorbency at 300 mu requires a spectro- 13.____
photometer sensitive in which one of the following spectral regions?

   A. Infra-red   B. Red
   C. Ultraviolet   D. Visible

14. Which of the following is NOT an oxidizing agent? 14.____

   A. Ceric sulfate   B. Citrate
   C. Ferricyanide   D. Permanganate

15. A buffer solution contains 15.____

   A. a strong acid   B. a weak acid or base
   C. an oxidizing agent D. sodium chloride

16. When a procedure calls for the d- or l-isomer of a substance, it may be possible to 16.____

   A. substitute the d- or l-isomer of a related substance
   B. use 1/2 the weight of a racemic mixture of the substance
   C. use twice the weight of the racemic mixture of the substance
   D. use the meso form of the substance

17. Hercuric ion will combine with which one of the following to form an undissociated salt? 17.____

   A. Carbonate   B. Chloride   C. Fluoride   D. Sulfate

18. pH is defined as 18.____

   A. $[H^+]$ B. $[H^+]+[OH^+]$
   C. $-\log[H^+]$ D. $2-\log[H^+]$

19. Which of the following can be used to prepare a pH standard? 19.____

   A. Acetate   B. Phosphate
   C. Potassium acid phthalate D. Veronal

20. The PREFERRED indicator to observe a pH change at 9.0 is 20.____

   A. bromthymol blue   B. methyl orange
   C. methyl red   D. phenolphthalein

21. The MOST effective buffer at pH of 6.8 is 21.____

   A. acetate   B. barbiturate
   C. borate   D. phosphate

22. The reaction involved in the titration of sodium oxalate by potassium permanganate is   22.____

    A. amphoteric titration   B. coulemetric titration
    C. neutralization   D. oxidation-reduction

23. Density is expressed BEST as   23.____

    A. mass/unit volume
    B. solubility per 100 ml
    C. specific gravity/unit volume
    D. volume/unit mass

24. 60° C converted to Fahrenheit is   24.____

    A. 110° F   B. 120° F   C. 130° F   D. 140° F

25. A substance with a melting point of $+28^\circ$ C at room temperature (25° C) will be a   25.____

    A. gas   B. liquid   C. mixture   D. solid

26. Which of the following has the HIGHEST boiling point?   26.____

    A. Acetic acid   B. Ethyl alcohol
    C. Methyl alcohol   D. Water

27. At constant pressure, which of the following will have the LOWEST freezing point?   27.____

    A. 0.1M NaCl   B. 0.2M NaCl
      0.1M Na_2HPO_4 C. 0.2M NaH_2PO_4

28. In one liter, a 5% solution contains _____ gm.   28.____

    A. 5   B. 25   C. 50   D. 100

29. Which one of the following compounds, in aqueous solution, absorbs ultraviolet light?   29.____

    A. Fumaric acid   B. Glutamic acid
    C. Malic acid   D. Succinic acid

30. Which of the following statements is LEAST likely to be correct?   30.____
Automated procedures

    A. are less costly than manual ones
    B. speed the rate of performance
    C. conserve laboratory space
    D. can be performed by less skilled personnel

31. The principle of the AutoAnalyzer is based on _____ analysis.   31.____

    A. sequential   B. discrete
    C. single   D. multiple

32. Atomic absorption is used to determine   32.____

    A. anions   B. atomic numbers
    C. cations   D. methyl groups

33. A nanogram of material is

    A. 1×10^{-3} g   B. 1×10^{-6} g
    C. 1×10^{-9} g   D. 1×10^{12} g

34. The Henderson-Hasselbalch equation is pH =

    A. $-\log[H]$ B. $\log[H]$

    C. $pK_a + \log \dfrac{[Acid]}{[Salt]}$ D. $pK_a + \log \dfrac{[Salt]}{[Acid]}$

35. In gas chromatography, the sample must be

    A. liquid   B. inorganic
    C. solid   D. volatilized

36. Atomic absorption spectroscopy requires

    A. an extremely hot flame   B. a hollow cathode lamp
    C. nuclear energy   D. vigorous mixing

37. Absolute temperature is _____ ° C.

    A. -100   B. -273   C. +100   D. +273

38. Gravimetric analysis PRIMARILY involves

    A. amperometric voltages   B. colorimetry
    C. titration   D. weighing

39. A gram molecular weight of a gas at standard conditions of temperature and pressure occupies _____ ml.

    A. 1,000   B. 10,000   C. 22,400   D. 44,800

40. Infra-red analysis is MOST often used in

    A. analytical chemistry   B. electrochemistry
    C. organic chemistry   D. physical chemistry

41. Enzymes are

    A. complex collagens   B. complex lipids
    C. polysaccharides   D. protein catalysts

42. Vitamin A is

    A. a nitrogenous compound   B. a protein catalyst
    C. water insoluble   D. water soluble

43. Which of the following is destroyed in pasteurization?

    A. Alkaline phosphatase   B. Calcium
    C. Iron binding protein   D. Lactose

44. In the human cell, energy is stored as   44.____

    A. adenosine monophosphate
    B. adenosine triphosphate
    C. creatine phosphokinase
    D. nicotine adenine dinucleotide

45. The acid found in normal gastric juice is   45.____

    A. citric   B. HCl   C. H_2SO_4 D. lactic

46. Albumin can be precipitated by addition of   46.____

    A. blood serum   B. sodium chloride
    C. sodium sulfate   D. water

47. Which of the following is NOT a reducing carbohydrate?   47.____

    A. Fructose   B. Galactose   C. Glucose   D. Sucrose

48. The kinetic theory of matter explains that   48.____

    A. the space between molecules of a gas is greater than the space occupied by the molecule itself
    B. molecules of matter do not move unless agitated
    C. molecules of matter are the ultimate particles of individual elements
    D. molecules of matter are always in motion

49. Of the following, the PRIMARY purpose of standards and controls is to obtain   49.____

    A. accuracy   B. priorities
    C. replicates   D. reproducibility

50. Of the following, the BEST definition for accuracy in laboratory practice is   50.____

    A. nearness to truth
    B. reproducibility of replicates
    C. within biological variation
    D. within 2 standard deviations of the mean

————

KEY (CORRECT ANSWERS)

1.	B	11.	C	21.	D	31.	A	41.	D
2.	C	12.	C	22.	D	32.	C	42.	C
3.	D	13.	C	23.	A	33.	C	43.	A
4.	D	14.	B	24.	D	34.	D	44.	B
5.	C	15.	B	25.	D	35.	D	45.	B
6.	D	16.	C	26.	A	36.	B	46.	C
7.	B	17.	B	27.	D	37.	B	47.	D
8.	B	18.	C	28.	C	38.	D	48.	D
9.	C	19.	C	29.	A	39.	C	49.	A
10.	C	20.	D	30.	D	40.	C	50.	A

TEST 2

DIRECTIONS: Each question or incomplete statement is followed by several suggested answers or completions. Select the one that BEST answers the question or completes the statement. *PRINT THE LETTER OF THE CORRECT ANSWER IN THE SPACE AT THE RIGHT.*

1. Which of the following formulas does NOT correspond to a known substance?   1.____

   A. $NaClO_2$ B. $NaPO_3$ C. $NaSO_2$ D. $Na_2S_2O_3$

2. In the reaction between zinc and concentrated nitric acid, shown UNBALANCED as   2.____
   ____Zn + ____HNO_3 = ____$Zn(NO_3)_2$ + ____NO + ____H_2O ,
   the number which should appear in front of the formula for nitric acid after the equation has been balanced is

   A. 3   B. 4   C. 6   D. 8

3. The element whose valence electrons have the quantum designation $4s^2$, $4p^5$ is No.   3.____

   A. 7   B. 25   C. 28   D. 35

4. In the case of the following equilibrium reaction, heat, which of the following actions will result in a CHANGE in the numerical value of the equilibrium constant?   4.____

   A. Addition of NO_2
   B. Increase in the temperature
   C. Increase in the total pressure
   D. Introduction of a catalyst

5. Of the following, the STRONGEST oxidizing agent is   5.____

   A. Br_2 B. F_2 C. Na D. O_2

6. The ionization constant of acetic acid is 1.8×10^{-5}. What is the pH of a liter of a solution containing 0.5 moles of acetic acid and 0.25 moles of sodium acetate?   6.____

   A. 1.8   B. 3.2   C. 4.44   D. 5.05

7. The volume of 0.42 M H_2SO_4 solution which will be EXACTLY neutralized by 230 ml of 0.70 M NaOH is   7.____

   A. 138   B. 192   C. 276   D. 384

8. Of the following, the substance which will NOT react with 1 M NaOH is   8.____

   A. Al   B. $AL(OH)_3$ C. Fe   D. SO_2

9. Of the following precipitates, the one which will NOT dissolve in 0.3 M HCl is   9.____

   A. As_2S_3 B. CuS C. $MnNH_4PO_4$ D. ZnS

10. The ionization constant, K_B, of ammonium hydroxide is 1.8×10^{-5}.   10.____
    What is the USEFUL range of pH's of the buffer solutions that can be made up from various mixtures of ammonium hydroxide and ammonium chloride?

    A. 8.5 to 10.5   B. 7 to 13   C. 5.5 to 7.5   D. 2 to 6

11. The atomic number of an element is equal to the 11._____

    A. number of neutrons in the nucleus
    B. number of protons in the nucleus
    C. sum of the protons and the electrons
    D. sum of the protons and the neutrons

12. What will be the APPROXIMATE increase in the reaction rate for every 10° C rise in temperature? 12._____
    _____ fold.

    A. 1.5   B. 2.0   C. 2.5   D. 3.0

13. At standard temperature and pressure, one liter of hydrogen gas contains APPROXI- 13._____
    MATELY the same number of molecules as

    A. 0.5 liter of oxygen
    B. 1.0 liter of sulfur dioxide
    C. 1.5 liters of ozone
    D. 2.0 liters of helium

14. The amount of $CuSO_4 . 5H_2O$ that must be dissolved in 100 ml of water to produce a 14._____
    solution containing 1 mg Cu^{++} per ml is _____ g.

    A. 0.100   B. 0.252   C. 0.393   D. 0.635

15. Of the following techniques, the one which would be the BEST to use in order to obtain 15._____
    absolute ethanol from the standard commercial product (95% ethanol, 5% water) is

    A. fractional distillation
    B. reaction with sodium, followed by distillation
    C. reaction with zinc, followed by filtration
    D. solvent extraction

16. Based upon mutual solubility considerations, which of the following would you expect to 16._____
    be the BEST solvent for a heavy machine oil?

    A. Acetone   B. Benzene   C. Dioxane   D. Ethanol

17. The specific gravity of concentrated hydrochloric acid reagent is 1.19. The solution con- 17._____
    tains 37% HCl.
    The molarity of the reagent is

    A. 2   B. 6   C. 8   D. 12

18. The purpose of a magnetic damper is to 18._____

    A. activate balance pans
    B. eliminate counting of swings
    C. keep the humidity down
    D. remove static electricity

19. Quantities of waste flammable organic liquids should be destroyed by   19.____
   A. burning under controlled conditions
   B. dumping in a secluded area
   C. evaporating on a water bath in a hood
   D. flushing down the sink

20. Of the following determinations, which would be BEST for routine use in the quality con-   20.____
   trol (i.e., testing of purity) of a solid benzene derivative?
   A. Diffusion coefficient   B. Melting range
   C. Solubility in toluene   D. Vapor pressure

21. The MEDIAN value in a column of figures is the_____ value.   21.____
   A. highest   B. lowest   C. mean   D. middle

22. The R_F in paper chromatography designates the   22.____
   A. distance between two solutes
   B. rate at which the fastest component migrates
   C. rate at which the slowest component migrates
   D. rate of solute migration compared to the solvent

23. An internal standard is used in flame photometry because it   23.____
   A. corrects for gas fluctuations
   B. forms a binary mixture
   C. increases the excitation
   D. simplifies calculations

24. In calcium analysis by atomic absorption, lanthanum is added to   24.____
   A. intensify the absorption
   B. intensify the emission
   C. prevent PO_4 interference
   D. reduce iron

25. The pressure of a mixture of three gases will be   25.____
   A. the product of the individual partial pressures
   B. the average of the partial pressures
   C. the sum of the partial pressures
   D. the partial pressure of the most volatile gas

26. Which of the following guides to the chemical literature deals EXCLUSIVELY with organic   26.____
   compounds?
   A. Abegg   B. Gmelin   C. Beilstein   D. Mellor

27. Of the following, the reagent which is employed in the separation and purification of   27.____
   ketones is
   A. Na_2CO_3 B. $NaHSO_3$ C. Cu_2C_{l2} D. $Ag(NH_3)_2OI$

47

28. Of the following, the compound which exists as two geometrical isomers is   28.____

   A. $HOOCCH=CH_2$ B. $HOOCCH_2CH_2COOH$
   C. $HOOCCH=CHCOOH$ D. $HOOCC=CH$

29. The monomer from which Teflon plastic is produced is   29.____

   A. $CF_2=CF_2$ B. CF_3COOH C. $CH_2=CH_2$ D. $CHF=CHF$

30. Of the following, the substance to start with in order to obtain the BEST yield of m-phe-   30.____
nylenediamine is

   A. aniline   B. benzenediazonium chloride
   C. m-dichlorophenol   D. m-dinitrobenzene

31. What is the MOST likely reason for a blood glucose to be exceedingly high (above 1000   31.____
mg per 100 ml)?
The

   A. patient ingested large amounts of carbohydrates
   B. patient ingested reducing substances
   C. patient was not fasting
   D. specimen was contaminated from an infusion

32. If the pH of blood plasma is 7.1 and the dissolved CO_2 is 2.0 mmoles, then the HCO_3 is   32.____
_____ mmoles.

   A. 10   B. 20   C. 30   D. 40

33. A triglyceride is a compound of three   33.____

   A. fatty acids
   B. fatty acids and one glycerol
   C. glycerols and one fatty acid
   D. glycerol molecules

34. Starch can be determined by measuring the intensity of the blue color when it reacts with   34.____

   A. alkaline copper   B. amylase
   C. iodine   D. silver

35. After the complete hydrolysis of lecithin, which of the following is NOT present?   35.____

   A. Choline   B. Ethanolamine
   C. Glycerol   D. Phosphoric acid

36. Fehling's Solution is used in the analysis of   36.____

   A. fat   B. protein
   C. reducing sugar   D. starch

37. An antimetabolite that inhibits an enzyme reaction is   37.____

   A. a heavy metal
   B. a substance that chelates with the substrate
   C. structurally related to the enzyme
   D. structurally related to the substrate

38. Of the following enzymes, the one that is NOT present in the carbohydrate citric acid cycle is

    A. fumarase
    B. isocitric dehydrogenase
    C. succinic dehydrogenase
    D. triose phosphate isomerase

38.____

39. The *xylose* test, as performed in the clinical laboratory, is a test for

    A. glomerular filtration   B. kidney function
    C. liver function   D. malabsorption

39.____

40. Serum acid phosphatase will be FALSELY elevated when the

    A. patient has urinary retention
    B. patient was not fasting
    C. serum alkaline phosphatase is elevated
    D. serum is hemolyzed

40.____

41. The *diurnal* variation of a blood substance infers that it varies with the

    A. age of the patient   B. procedure used
    C. sex of the patient   D. time of day

41.____

42. A single peak in the Tiselius electrophoresis indicates that the

    A. substance is a pure protein
    B. substance is not a protein
    C. solution contains mucopolysaccharides
    D. solution is a mixture of proteins

42.____

43. 68 ml. of gastric juice were titrated to pH 7.0 and found to contain 138 mmoles per liter of acid.
What is the acidity in mmoles of the total volume of gastric juice?

    A. 20.3   B. 14.4   C. 9.4   D. 4.9

43.____

44. The glucose oxidase method for blood glucose is PREFERRED over any other blood glucose test because

    A. it is the fastest procedure
    B. it requires the least expensive reagents
    C. the reagents are readily stable
    D. there is no interference from other reducing substances

44.____

45. Fluoride is used as a blood anticoagulant for glucose determinations because it

    A. inhibits bacterial growth
    B. inhibits glycolytic enzymes
    C. precipitates calcium
    D. prevents hemolysis

45.____

49

46. Deoxyribonucleoproteins form viscous solutions because they   46._____

    A. are elongated
    B. are spherical
    C. contain protein
    D. have a high molecular weight

47. Bromsulphonphthalein (BSP) is used as a liver function test because the dye is   47._____

    A. excreted by the kidney   B. excreted by the liver
    C. not adsorbed to proteins   D. stored in the liver

48. Proteins will NOT migrate in an electric field at _____ pH.   48._____

    A. a neutral   B. an acid
    C. an alkaline   D. an isoelectric

49. A pooled serum may be used as a   49._____

    A. daily control   B. gas analysis control
    C. primary standard   D. secondary standard

50. Which of the following is NOT a hormone?   50._____

    A. Carotene   B. Estriol
    C. Epinephrine   D. Secretin

KEY (CORRECT ANSWERS)

1. C	11. B	21. D	31. B	41. D
2. D	12. B	22. D	32. D	42. A
3. D	13. B	23. A	33. A	43. C
4. B	14. C	24. C	34. A	44. D
5. B	15. B	25. C	35. C	45. C
6. C	16. B	26. C	36. C	46. D
7. B	17. D	27. B	37. C	47. C
8. C	18. B	28. C	38. B	48. D
9. B	19. C	29. A	39. B	49. B
10. A	20. B	30. D	40. C	50. A

TEST 3

DIRECTIONS: Each question or incomplete statement is followed by several suggested answers or completions. Select the one that BEST answers the question or completes the statement. *PRINT THE LETTER OF THE CORRECT ANSWER IN THE SPACE AT THE RIGHT.*

1. One liter is APPROXIMATELY one   1.____

   A. pint   B. quart
   C. half-gallon   D. gallon

2. The temperature on the Kelvin (absolute) scale which corresponds to -60° C is   2.____

   A. -333   B. +213   C. +273   D. +333

3. How many liters of H_2 at STP would be displaced from 500 ml of 4M HCl by excess zinc?   3.____

   A. 11.2   B. 22.4   C. 44.8   D. 89.6

4. Metallic sodium should be stored in   4.____

   A. alcohol   B. kerosene   C. sawdust   D. water

5. The reaction,   5.____

$MnO_2 + H^+ + H_2C_2O_4 \rightarrow CO_2 + H_2O + MN^{++}$, is not balanced.
After balancing it, select, of the following, the CORRECT number of moles of $H_2C_2O_4$ required to react with one mole of MnO_2.

   A. 1/2   B. 1   C. 2   D. 4

6. The pH of .01M HCl is   6.____

   A. 10^{-2} B. 1   C. 2   D. 3

7. The ionization constant of acetic acid is 1.8×10^{-5}. The hydrogen ion concentration in a solution of 0.5M acetic acid and 0.5M sodium acetate is   7.____

   A. $.9 \times 10^{-5}$M   B. 1.8×10^{-5}M
   C. 3×10^{-3}M   D. 3.3×10^{-12}M

8. A 50.0 ml sample of NaOH solution requires exactly 27.8 ml of 0.100M acid in titration. What is the normality of the NaOH?   8.____

   A. 0.0278   B. 0.0556   C. 0.112   D. 0.556

9. The solubility of $Pb(IO_3)_2$ in water is 4.0×10^{-5} moles/ liter. What is the K_{sp} (solubility product) for $Pb(IO_3)_2$?   9.____

   A. 1.6×10^{-9} B. 2.4×10^{-13}
   C. 4.0×10^{-5} D. 12×10^{-5}

10. Light of 5000 Å wave length   10.____

    A.   is in the ultraviolet region
    B.   is in the visible region
    C.   contains twice as much energy as light of 2500 Å wave length
    D.   is in the infra-red region

11. The compound Na_2S contains what percentage S?   11.____

    A. 33%   B. 41%   C. 59%   D. 69%

12. A compound that has the power to neutralize an acid and form a salt is called a(n)   12.____

    A. buffer   B. hetone   C. anhydride   D. alkali

13. Which of the following isotopes is NOT radioactive?   13.____

    A. C^{12} B. C^{14} C. Co^{60} D. H^3

14. The organic compound C_4H_{10} 14.____

    A.   is a unique compound with no isomers
    B.   exists in two isomeric forms
    C.   exists in three isomeric forms
    D.   exists in many (more than three) isomeric forms

15. Of the following, the STRONGEST reducing agent is _____ acid.   15.____

    A. acetic   B. nitric   C. oxalic   D. phosphoric

16. Which of the following solutions has the LOWEST freezing point?   16.____
    IM

    A. calcium sulfate   B. calcium chloride
    C. sodium chloride   D. sugar

17. The general formula for an organic aldehyde is   17.____

    A. RCHO   B. RCOOH   C. RCOR   D. ROR

Questions 18-19.

DIRECTIONS: Questions 18 and 19 are to be answered on the basis of the following reversible reaction.

$$N_2O_4 \text{ (gas)} \rightleftarrows 2NO_2 \text{ (gas)}$$

18. Which expression CORRECTLY describes the equilibrium constant? (P stands for pressure)   18.____

    A. $P_{N_2O_4}/P^2_{NO_2}$ B. $P^2_{NO_2}/P_{N_2O_4}$

    C. $P_{NO_2}/P_{N_2O_4}$ D. $2(P_{NO_2})/P_{N_2O_4}$

19. If the total pressure on the reaction at equilibrium is suddenly increased at constant temperature,   19.____

    A. nothing would happen
    B. the equilibrium constant would change
    C. the reaction would shift toward NO_2 (gas)
    D. the reaction would shift toward N_2O_4 (gas)

20. A reaction requires 1 hour to run to completion at 30° C. The same reaction will run to   20.____
completion in 15 minutes at APPROXIMATELY _____ $^\circ$ C.

    A. 20   B. 40   C. 50   D. 120

21. A quality control chart is used to   21.____

    A. check day-to-day variability
    B. define the laboratory accuracy
    C. define the laboratory workload
    D. find normal values

22. A primary standard is prepared by   22.____

    A. dilution of a solution
    B. always using oxidizing agents
    C. weighing on a gross balance
    D. weighing on an analytical balance

23. What part of a population will be included within 2 standard deviation in a normal distribution curve?   23.____
_____ percent.

    A. 65   B. 75   C. 85   D. 95

24. When a frozen control material is thawing and a portion is taken before complete melting   24.____
and mixing, the obtained values are LIKELY to be

    A. high   B. low   C. unchanged   D. variable

25. The PROPER use of a volumetric pipette requires   25.____

    A. allowing it to drain   B. blowing it out
    C. washing it out   D. weighing the contents

26. When the skin is splashed with acid, it should   26.____

    A. immediately be covered with oil
    B. immediately be flushed with water
    C. immediately be flushed with weak acid
    D. not be touched

27. Fume hoods are used in laboratories to   27.____

    A. allow the use of a flame
    B. exhaust noxious fumes
    C. provide a well-lit work area
    D. provide storage space

28. How many milligrams of nitrogen are there in 40 milligrams of urea?   28.____

     A.   16.8   B.   18.5   C.   21.6   D.   24.6

29. The presence of barbiturates in a blood sample can BEST be determined by   29.____

     A.   cellulose acetate electrophoresis
     B.   fractional distillation
     C.   paper electrophoresis
     D.   thin layer chromatography

30. Urease is a(n)   30.____

     A.   major constituent of urine
     B.   nucleic acid metabolite
     C.   protein metabolite
     D.   enzyme

31. The MAJOR urinary excretory product of steroid metabolism is   31.____

     A.   cholesterol   B.   estrogen
     C.   17-ketosteroids   D.   lanosteroid

32. The MAJOR polysaccharide involved in human metabolism is   32.____

     A.   a-amylopectin   B.   amylose
     C.   glycogen   D.   starch

33. The chemical identification of glucose can be made by the formation of a   33.____

     A.   boron bead
     B.   complex with bathophenanthrolene
     C.   phenylhydrazine
     D.   polymer

34. Which of the following has an asymmetric carbon atom?   34.____
     _____ acid.

     A.   Acetic   B.   Lactic   C.   Oleic   D.   Succinic

35. Nitrogen is NOT present in   35.____

     A.   glucuronic acid   B.   glutathione
     C.   glycolic acid   D.   glycine

36. The MAJOR intracellular ion is   36.____

     A.   calcium   B.   carbonate   C.   potassium   D.   sodium

37. The blood volume in a normal adult approximates _____ ml.   37.____

     A.   1000   B.   3000   C.   5000   D.   8000

38. The pH of normal blood is   38.____

     A.   6.40   B.   6.90   C.   7.40   D.   7.90

39. The serum protein involved in the clotting of blood is

    A. fibrinogen   B. 1-globulin
    C. 2-globulin   D. haptoglobin

39.____

40. Which one of the following tests can NOT be done on oxalated blood plasma?

    A. Calcium   B. Creatinine   C. Glucose   D. Urine

40.____

41. The nitrogen content of proteins is MOST NEARLY _____ percent.

    A. 16.5   B. 18.5   C. 20.5   D. 22.5

41.____

42. Protein-bound iodine is a measure of _____ function.

    A. adrenal   B. cardiac   C. liver   D. thyroid

42.____

43. Which of the following is NOT a liver function test?

    A. Cephalin flocculation   B. Glucose tolerance
    C. Serum bilirubin   D. Thymol turbidity

43.____

44. Heparin is often used as a(n)

    A. anticoagulant
    B. chelating agent in Ca^{++} analysis
    C. colored complex
    D. primary standard

44.____

45. Amino acids are bound together to form a protein through

    A. alcohol acid esters   B. glycosidic linkages
    C. peptide bonds   D. 3'5' phosphate bonds

45.____

46. Inulin is a polysaccharide of

    A. fructose   B. galactose   C. glucose   D. lactose

46.____

47. A characteristic of isoenzymes is that

    A. the enzymes have identical activities at a given pH
    B. the protein moieties have the same charge densities
    C. the protein moieties have the same molecular weight
    D. a substrate is common to all the enzymes

47.____

48. The MOST likely journal to contain articles about elemental analysis is

    A. Analytical Chemistry
    B. Clinical Chemistry
    C. Journal of Chromatography
    D. Journal of Organic Chemistry

48.____

49. The Index Medicus contains

    A. abstracts of journal articles
    B. information about disease
    C. information about drugs
    D. references to journal articles by subject and author

49.____

50. When it is necessary to refer to published articles in the field of chemistry when only the 50.____
subject is known, the BEST source of reference is

    A. CHEMICAL ABSTRACTS
    B. INDEX OF AMERICAN CHEMICAL SOCIETY
    C. INDEX OF CLINICAL CHEMISTRY
    D. INDEX MEDICUS

KEY (CORRECT ANSWERS)

1. B	11. B	21. A	31. B	41. D
2. B	12. D	22. D	32. B	42. C
3. B	13. A	23. D	33. B	43. A
4. B	14. B	24. D	34. C	44. A
5. B	15. C	25. A	35. B	45. C
6. C	16. B	26. B	36. C	46. D
7. B	17. A	27. B	37. D	47. C
8. B	18. B	28. C	38. C	48. A
9. B	19. D	29. A	39. A	49. D
10. B	20. C	30. D	40. B	50. A

EXAMINATION SECTION

TEST 1

DIRECTIONS: Each question or incomplete statement is followed by several suggested answers or completions. Select the one that BEST answers the question or completes the statement. *PRINT THE LETTER OF THE CORRECT ANSWER IN THE SPACE AT THE RIGHT.*

1. Cyanocobalamin Co-57 is used in which of the following ways?　　　　1.＿＿＿
   A. In diagnosis of pernicious anemia
   B. In tumor localization
   C. As an antineoplastic agent
   D. As an antineoplastic agent
   E. In RBC survival time determination

2. Cyanocobalamin is a member of which of the following classes?　　　　2.＿＿＿
   A. Glycosides　　　　B. Alkaloids　　　　C. Hormones
   D. Vitamins　　　　E. Enzymes

3. The phenothiazine derivative with the structure shown at the right is BEST characterized as a(n)　　　　3.＿＿＿
   A. antipsychotic agent
   B. tricyclic antidepressant
   C. antihistamine
   D. non-narcotic analgesic

4. Which of the following drugs is a steroid?　　　　4.＿＿＿
   A. Reserpine　　　　B. Hydrocortisone　　　　C. Pentobarbital
   D. Diazepam　　　　E. Indomethacin

5. In cases of phenobarbital overdosage, the rate of excretion of the drug may be increased by　　　　5.＿＿＿
   A. administering ammonium chloride I.V.
   B. administering calcium chloride solution I.V.
   C. acidifying the urione
   D. administering sodium bicarbonate solution I.V.
   E. administering sodium biphosphate solution I.V.

6. Digoxin belongs to which of the following classes?　　　　6.＿＿＿
   A. Glycosides　　　　B. Terpenes　　　　C. Carbohydrates
   D. Alkaloids　　　　E. Proteins

7. An I.V. admixture called for the addition of chlorpromazine hydrochloride injection and sodium pentobarbital injection.
Which of the following would occur?
   A. The color of the solution would change.
   B. A gas would evolve.
   C. A precipitate would form.
   D. The temperature of the solution would noticeably change.
   E. No reaction would occur.

7.____

8. The form of radioactivity that is LEAST damaging to human tissue as an external source of radiation is
   A. alpha   B. beta   C. gamma   D. delta   E. epsilon

8.____

9. Propylparaben is employed in pharmaceutical preparations as a(n)
   A. suspending agent   B. buffering agent
   C. antioxidant   D. preservative
   E. surfactant

9.____

10. Exposure to light in the presence of organic matter causes silver nitrate solution to
    A. turn brown due to the formation of nitrogen oxides
    B. turn grayish black due to the formation of metallic silver
    C. form a white precipitate due to the formation of silver chloride
    D. form a white precipitate due to the formation of silver carbonate
    E. remain colorless due to the formation of a soluble complex with protein

10.____

KEY (CORRECT ANSWERS)

1.	A	6.	A
2.	D	7.	C
3.	A	8.	A
4.	B	9.	D
5.	D	10.	B

TEST 2

DIRECTIONS: Each question or incomplete statement is followed by several suggested answers or completions. Select the one that BEST answers the question or completes the statement. *PRINT THE LETTER OF THE CORRECT ANSWER IN THE SPACE AT THE RIGHT.*

1. Unaltered red blood cells labeled with Cr-51 are used to study   11.____
   A. hepatic function   B. red blood cell volume
   C. cardiovascular function   D. pancreatic function
   E. blood pooling

2. Antacids which are devoid of systemic effects may be characterized as   12.____
   A. salts of carbonic acid
   B. compounds which are insoluble in water
   C. sodium salts of weak acids
   D. compounds which are well dissociated in water
   E. hydroxy derivatives of transition metal ions

3. Acidification of the urine of a patient taking aspirin can be expected to   13.____
   A. increase the rate of excretion of the drug
   B. increase the blood level of the drug
   C. cause hydrolysis of the drug
   D. lower the blood level of the drug
   E. have no effect on the excretion of the drug

4. Which of the following is sufficiently volatile to undergo a reduction in potency   14.____
when exposed to air?
   A. Glyceryl trinitrate   B. Diazepam
   C. Amphetamine sulfate   D. Glutethimide
   E. Propoxyphene napsylate

5. The diagnostic tool used to determine thyroid function is radioactive   15.____
   A. cobalt   B. gold   C. iodine
   D. chromium   E. strontium

6. Ethanol is present in anesthetic ether for which of the following reasons? It   16.____
   A. prevents formation of peroxide
   B. lowers the vapor pressure
   C. raises the boiling point
   D. neutralizes acidic decomposition products by forming an ester
   E. is a non-removable contaminant resulting from synthesis of ether

Questions 7-8.

DIRECTIONS: Questions 7 and 8 are to be answered on the basis of the following chart.

Epinephrine

7. Aqueous solutions of epinephrine at neutral to alkaline pH will tend to develop   17.____
a pink color. The color is due to
    A. precipitation of epinephrine
    B. coupling of two molecules of epinephrine
    C. oxidation of the catechol nucleus
    D. chelate formation
    E. oxidation of the amino group

8. Aqueous solutions of epinephrine should be stabilized by   18.____
    A. keeping the pH acidic only
    B. keeping the pH acidic and adding sodium bisulfite
    C. keeping the pH alkaline only
    D. keeping the pH alkaline and adding sodium bisulfite
    E. adding trace amounts of transition metal ions

9. Dissolution refers to which of the following processes?   19.____
    A. A solute coming out of solution
    B. A substance going into solution
    C. An increases in solubility caused by temperature increase
    D. Common ion effect in causing a substance to go into solution
    E. The process of fractional crystallization

10. A sulfonamide with the general structure shown   20.____
at the right does which of the following? It $H_2N - \langle \bigcirc \rangle - SO_2\text{-}NH\text{-}R$
    A. acts as inhibitors of acetylcholinesterase
    B. blocks the action of vitamin B_6
    C. inhibits the incorporation of PABA into folic acid
    D. inhibits the action of cyclic AMP
    E. blocks the action of insulin

_____

KEY (CORRECT ANSWERS)

1.	B	6.	A
2.	B	7.	C
3.	B	8.	B
4.	A	9.	B
5.	C	10.	C

_____

EXAMINATION SECTION
TEST 1

DIRECTIONS: Each question or incomplete statement is followed by several suggested answers or completions. Select the one that BEST answers the question or completes the statement. *PRINT THE LETTER OF THE CORRECT ANSWER IN THE SPACE AT THE RIGHT.*

1. Which of the following is NOT a derivative of opium?   1._____

    A. Cocaine   B. Heroin
    C. Codeine   D. Morphine

2. Complete the following statement.   2._____
    Morphine is APPROXIMATELY _____ times as potent as opium.

    A. 2   B. 5   C. 10   D. 25

3. Approximately when was the hypodermic needle invented?   3._____

    A. 1450   B. 1660   C. 1840   D. 1910

4. What was the prevalent euphemism for narcotic addiction after the Civil War?   4._____

    A. *Barbary plague*   B. *Hay fever*
    C. *Soldier's illness*   D. *Hash head*

5. Which of the following terms does NOT describe a form of oral opium ingestion?   5._____

    A. Dover's powder   B. Laudanum
    C. Paregoric   D. Gold dust

6. When was heroin synthesized from opium?   6._____

    A. 1719   B. 1898   C. 1913   D. 1927

7. Which of the following 19th century literary artists was NOT known to be an opium user?   7._____

    A. Edgar Allan Poe   B. Thomas de Quincey
    C. Samuel Coleridge   D. Alfred Lord Tennyson

8. Of the following groups of drugs, which provide(s) the MAIN causes of abuse among   8._____
    adults?
        I. Narcotics
       II. Sedatives
     III. Tranquilizers
     IV. Stimulants
      V. Hallucinogens
    The CORRECT answer is:

    A. II *only*   B. I, V
    C. III, IV   D. II,III, IV

9. Fill in the blank with the appropriate letter.   9._____
    _____ are drugs which produce insensibility or stupor due to their depressant effect on the central nervous system.

    A. Sedatives   B. Tranquilizers
    C. Narcotics   D. Hallucinogens

10. Which of the following should NOT be classed as a narcotic?   10.____

    A. Heroin   B. Morphine   C. Cocaine   D. Marijuana

11. Which one of the following is NOT a synthetic opiate?   11.____

    A. Meperidine   B. Dimethyltryptamine
    C. Oxycodone   D. Methadone

12. A drug which affects the nervous system will ALWAYS effect a change in   12.____

    A. breathing   B. emotional responses
    C. pupil dilation   D. intellectual processes

13. Which term represents the body's ability to adapt to the presence of a foreign sub-   13.____
stance?

    A. Abstinence syndrome   B. Dependence
    C. Tolerance   D. Habituation

14. TRUE OR FALSE?   14.____
Tolerance can occur without physical dependence.

    A. True   B. False
    C. More often true   D. More often false

Questions 15-17.

DIRECTIONS: Match the number in Column A with the corresponding letter of its definition in
Column B.

COLUMN A	COLUMN B	
15. Habituation	A. A condition resulting from the repeated consumption of a drug, which involves little or no evidence of tolerance, some psychological dependence, and a desire (not compulsion) to continue taking the drug for the feeling of well-being it produces	15.____
16. Addiction	B. A state of periodic or chronic intoxication produced by the repeated consumption of a drug; involves tolerance, psychological dependence, usually physical dependence, and an overwhelming compulsion to continue using the drug	16.____
17. Drug dependence	C. A state arising from the repeated administration of a drug on a periodic or continuous basis	17.____

18. Which drug is the standard of pain relief by which other narcotic analgesics are evalu-   18.____
ated?

    A. Heroin   B. Morphine   C. Codeine   D. Demurol

19. Which of the following is NOT a side effect of opiates?   19.____

    A. Nausea   B. Itching
    C. Flushing   D. Pupil dilation

20. Symptoms of withdrawal from narcotic analgesics are: 20.____
Nervousness, anxiety, sleeplessness
Yawning, running eyes and nose, sweating
Enlargement of the pupils, *gooseflesh, muscle-twitching*
Severe aches of back and legs, hot and cold flashes
Vomiting and diarrhea
Increase in breathing rate, blood pressure, and temperature
A feeling of desperation and an obsessional desire to secure a *fix*

Which one of the following statements concerning withdrawal is FALSE?

    A. Symptoms occur 8 to 12 hours after the last dose.
    B. The intensity of withdrawal symptoms vary with the degree of *psychological dependence.*
    C. Symptoms reach a peak between 36 to 72 hours after last dose.
    D. Symptoms are present for up to two weeks afterward.

21. About what percent of a heroin *bag* actually contains heroin?   21.____

    A. 10-18%   B. 1-3%   C. 3-10%   D. 20-30%

22. In which of the following cases would barbiturates NOT be prescribed?   22.____

    A. Fatigue   B. Epilepsy
    C. Insomnia   D. High blood pressure

23. The combination of which of the following pairs will MOST likely cause death?   23.____

    A. Alcohol and aspirin   B. Marijuana and barbiturates
    C. Alcohol and marijuana   D. Alcohol and barbiturates

24. Which of the following traits BEST characterize(s) the barbiturate abuser?   24.____

    A. Friendly and outgoing   B. Energetic
    C. Motivated   D. Slurred speech

25. Which of these drugs is addictive?   25.____

    A. Mescaline   B. Amphetamines
    C. Barbiturates   D. LSD

KEY (CORRECT ANSWERS)

1.	A		11.	B
2.	C		12.	B
3.	C		13.	C
4.	C		14.	A
5.	D		15.	A
6.	B		16.	B
7.	D		17.	C
8.	D		18.	B
9.	C		19.	D
10.	D		20.	B

21.	C
22.	A
23.	D
24.	D
25.	C

———

TEST 2

DIRECTIONS: Each question or incomplete statement is followed by several suggested answers or completions. Select the one that BEST answers the question or completes the statement. *PRINT THE LETTER OF THE CORRECT ANSWER IN THE SPACE AT THE RIGHT.*

1. The hallucinations of barbiturate withdrawal are similar to those of   1.____

    A. opium euphoria
    B. delirium tremens of alcoholism
    C. marijuana *highs*
    D. hallucinations from LSD

2. TRUE OR FALSE?   2.____
The anti-psychotic tranquilizers can produce physical dependence.

    A. False   B. True
    C. Sometimes true   D. More often false

3. Which of the following is NOT a non-barbiturate depressant?   3.____

    A. Glutethimide   B. Ethchlorvynol
    C. Phenobarbitol   D. Methyprylon

4. Where is cocaine to be PRINCIPALLY found?   4.____

    A. South America   B. Turkey
    C. Southeast Asia   D. Afghanistan

5. What was cocaine's PRINCIPAL medical use in recent years?   5.____

    A. Treatment of narcolepsy   B. Local anesthetic
    C. Depressant   D. Stimulant

6. Which of the following is NOT a result of cocaine use?   6.____

    A. Excitability
    B. Reduction of blood pressure
    C. Pupil dilation
    D. Depression

7. Which of the following is a characteristic of cocaine use?   7.____

    A. Hallucinations   B. Addiction
    C. Tolerance   D. Withdrawal

8. What were amphetamines FIRST used for?   8.____

    A. Curb appetites
    B. Relieve depression
    C. Narcolepsy treatment
    D. Nasal vasoconstrictor for colds and hay fever

9. Which of the following is NOT a proper use for amphetamines?   9.____

    A. Fight drowsiness
    B. Oppose starvation
    C. Calm hyperactive children
    D. Treat senility

10. TRUE OR FALSE?   10.____
Amphetamine drugs with the exception of methamphetamine seldom cause death,
even in acute overdosage.

    A. True   B. False
    C. Cannot be proved   D. Does not apply

11. Amphetamines do NOT cause   11.____

    A. sweating   B. rise in blood pressure
    C. dry mouth   D. slower heartbeat

12. Which of the following is characteristic of amphetamine use?   12.____

    A. Tolerance development   B. Abstinence syndrome
    C. Physical dependence   D. Placidity

13. Which term among the following does NOT belong with the others?   13.____

    A. Physiometrics   B. Psychotomimetrics
    C. Dysleptics   D. Hallucinogens

14. Which one of the following hallucinogens was NOT used by the Indians in Mexico and   14.____
the American Southwest?

    A. Mescaline   B. Peyote
    C. Psilocybin   D. LSD

15. Complete the following analogy: 15.____
Peyote: cactus :: psilocybin :

    A. desert   B. crystals
    C. mushroom   D. hallucinogen

16. When was LSD FIRST synthesized?   16.____

    A. 1919   B. 1958   C. 1938   D. 1965

17. LSD's character is   17.____

    A. bitter, pungent, colorless
    B. bitter, odorless, colorless
    C. tasteless, pungent, white powder
    D. tasteless, odorless, colorless

18. Which effect USUALLY characterizes LSD?   18.____

    A. Central nervous system reaction
    B. Withdrawal
    C. Intense psychic dependence
    D. Physical dependence

19. The PRIMARY reason for advising someone NOT to use LSD and other hallucinogens at   19.____
    this time is that

    A. it is likely to damage chromosomes
    B. it is against the law
    C. the possible psychological effects of the hallucinogen may be very harmful to the
       individual's mental health
    D. he probably will use other drugs as well

20. The inhalation of glue, rubber cement, paint thinner, and other solvents will be MOST   20.____
    harmful to which part of the body?
    The

    A. heart   B. liver   C. kidney   D. brain

21. The abuse of solvents does NOT cause   21.____

    A. unconsciousness   B. addiction
    C. psychic dependence   D. tolerance

22. Which one of the following symptoms is NOT that of solvent abuse?   22.____

    A. Blurry vision   B. Ringing ears
    C. Drowsiness   D. Staggering

23. Which one of the following is NOT an after-effect of solvent intoxication?   23.____

    A. Lack of memory   B. Drowsiness
    C. Stupor   D. Exhilaration

24. TRUE OR FALSE?   24.____
    Suffocation is the CHIEF danger of solvent inhalation.

    A. True   B. False
    C. Sometimes true   D. Cannot tell

25. TRUE OR FALSE?   25.____
    A severe type of anemia has been observed in glue-sniffers who have an inherited
    defect of the blood cells.

    A. True   B. False
    C. Sometimes false   D. Impossible to decide

KEY (CORRECT ANSWERS)

1.	B		11.	D
2.	A		12.	A
3.	C		13.	A
4.	A		14.	D
5.	B		15.	C
6.	B		16.	C
7.	A		17.	D
8.	D		18.	A
9.	B		19.	C
10.	A		20.	B

21.	B
22.	C
23.	D
24.	A
25.	A

———

TEST 3

DIRECTIONS: Each question or incomplete statement is followed by several suggested answers or completions. Select the one that BEST answers the question or completes the statement. *PRINT THE LETTER OF THE CORRECT ANSWER IN THE SPACE AT THE RIGHT.*

1. TRUE OR FALSE?
    The marijuana plant can be used for the manufacture of twine, rope, bags, clothing, and paper.

A. True	B. False
C. Sometimes true	D. Undecided

    1.____

2. The drug that is NOT from the cannabis sativa plant is

    A. marijuana   B. LSD   C. THC   D. hashish

    2.____

3. Habitual use of marijuana will NOT lead to

    A. physical dependence
    B. pre-occupation with marijuana use
    C. lethargy
    D. self-neglect

    3.____

4. Which of the following is NOT caused by the use of marijuana?

A. Loss of memory	B. Psychotic episodes
C. Anti-social behavior	D. Temperature change

    4.____

5. The MOST harmful possible effect on a user of marijuana would be

    A. its deleterious nature
    B. social aspersion
    C. the inherent consequence of *moving up* to more dangerous drugs
    D. the facilitation of association with groups involved with dangerous drugs

    5.____

6. In comparison to the harmful effects of alcohol, marijuana is BEST described as

    A. equally bad
    B. used by *lower-type* people
    C. less harmful physically
    D. more harmful physically

    6.____

7. The relation of marijuana to harder narcotic drugs that has validity is that

    A. there is a causal relationship between marijuana and harder drugs
    B. while there is no causal link, almost all heroin addicts started with drugs by smoking marijuana
    C. most marijuana smokers will graduate to harder drugs
    D. marijuana smokers are usually forced to harder drugs by their tolerance to marijuana in order to achieve the same *high*

    7.____

8. The use of harder narcotic drugs, e.g., heroin, is confined to   8.____
          I.   college campus
          II. slum areas in cities
          III. suburbia
          IV. areas of war
          V.   rural areas
    The CORRECT answer is:

    A. I, II, IV   B. II, IV
    C. I, II, III, IV   D. I, II, III, IV, V

9. Listed below are causes of drug addiction in an inner city slum area. You are to arrange   9.____
    them in order of priority of cause from MOST important to LEAST important.
          I.   Slum conditions
          II. Access to drugs
          III. Need to make money
          IV. Feeling of hopelessness
    The CORRECT answer is:

    A. I, IV,II,III   B. II, III, I, IV
    C. IV, III, II, I   D. III, II, IV, I

10. Of the following causes, which would NOT, in all probability, lead to drug addiction in an   10.____
    individual?

    A. Emotional instability
    B. Inability or unwillingness to face the responsibility of maturity
    C. Inability to develop meaningful interpersonal relationships
    D. Need to be the best and to compete very hard to get to the top

11. The FIRST contacts with drug use on the part of the teenager are usually for the purpose   11.____
    of

    A. learning the real meaning of life
    B. being social and friendly
    C. heightening sensations
    D. loosening inhibitions

12. In general, it can be said that there are three types of drug users: 12.____
          1.   the situational, e.g., the housewife who uses amphetamines to curb weight;
          2.   the *spree* users who use drugs occasionally for kicks or experience which is usu
               ally done in groups; and
          3.   the hard core addict.
    Of the following situations, which one BEST describes the definite transition from (1) or
    (2) to (3); i.e., from occasional user to addict?

    A. Your contacts and friends start using hard drugs.
    B. Depression takes hold of you while you are using drugs occasionally.
    C. Interaction between drug effects and personality causes a loss of control over drug
        use.
    D. The occasional user becomes so accustomed to using drugs that it becomes a
        way of life.

13. Approximately what percent of heroin addicts return to the drug after withdrawal has been effected?   13.____

    A. 50%   B. 70%   C. 80%   D. 90%

14. Until recent years, drug treatment consisted only of   14.____

    A. psychiatric evaluation
    B. counseling upon return to the community
    C. withdrawal
    D. the methadone treatment

15. Which of the following organizations has started *halfway* houses to help drug addicts adjust to living without drugs?   15.____

    A. American Medical Association
    B. Phoenix House
    C. Weight Watchers, Inc.
    D. Alcoholics Anonymous

16. The approach of the United States government and state and local government towards drug abuse can BEST be described as   16.____

    A. compassionate
    B. similar to that of the British
    C. punitive
    D. effective

17. Which one of the following BEST describes the *British System for* treating addiction?   17.____

    A. Strict law enforcement
    B. Allowing physicians to issue maintenance doses if withdrawal endangers the patient's health
    C. Taxing drugs heavily without outlawing their use
    D. Putting addicts in jail until they no longer need drugs

18. Which Federal agency oversees programs for treating drug abuse?   18.____

    A. National Institute of Mental Health
    B. Federal Bureau of Narcotics and Dangerous Drugs
    C. United States Customs Service
    D. Federal Bureau of Investigation

19. A recognizable symptom of drug abuse is   19.____

    A. the use of abusive language
    B. changes in behavior out of character with a person's previous conduct
    C. querulousness
    D. frustration

20. If one observes irritation of mucous membranes in the mouth and nose and excessive nasal secretions combined with heavy breath odor, the subject might be a   20.____

    A. glue sniffer   B. amphetamine user
    C. marijuana smoker   D. LSD user

21. The symptoms of alcohol intoxication are similar to the drug intoxication of   21.____

    A. cocaine   B. marijuana
    C. amphetamines   D. barbiturates

22. If one is observed to be highly nervous, irritable, argumentative, accompanied by   22.____
extreme dryness of mouth and nose, this person could be using

    A. barbiturates   B. amphetamines
    C. mescaline   D. narcotics

23. Which disease is MOST likely to be communicated from the use of unsterile hypodermic   23.____
needles?

    A. Hepatitis   B. Sleeping sickness
    C. Dysentery   D. Diphtheria

24. What is the relevant Federal law for controlling illicit narcotics traffic?   24.____

    A. Uniform Commercial Code   B. Smith Act
    C. Harrison Act   D. Stamp Act

25. What is the relevant Federal law for controlling traffic in depressants and stimulants?   25.____

    A. Drug Abuse Control Amendment of 1965
    B. Drug Rehabilitation Act of 1971
    C. Uniform Narcotic Law
    D. Marijuana Tax Act of 1937

KEY (CORRECT ANSWERS)

1.	A		11.	B
2.	B		12.	C
3.	A		13.	D
4.	D		14.	C
5.	D		15.	B
6.	C		16.	C
7.	B		17.	B
8.	D		18.	A
9.	A		19.	B
10.	D		20.	A

21.	D
22.	B
23.	A
24.	C
25.	A

POLICE SCIENCE NOTES

BASIC FUNDAMENTALS OF DRUGS FOR THE POLICE OFFICER

CONTENTS

POLICE SCIENCE NOTES
BASIC FUNDAMENTALS OF DRUGS FOR THE POLICE OFFICER

I. INTRODUCTION

The fact that drug addiction and drug abuse are closely connected with crime need not be explored here. However, it is very useful for the police officer to be aware of the classifications of the various types of drugs that are abused, the physical forms the drugs can have, and the ways they affect the user under varying conditions. All such information can sharpen the crime scene investigator's perception of physical evidence that is associated with illegal use of drugs. This section summarizes this type of information insofar as it seems useful for the purposes of crime scene search.

Some police officers mistakenly believe that the term "narcotic" covers all the controlled drugs and frequently use the term in this manner. Narcotic drugs are only those of addiction which are extracted from the opium plant and the leaves of the coca shrub.

The term *controlled drugs* is generally understood to include all drugs which are covered by law and are restricted in some manner. Because of the technical requirements of the courts it is better that the term *controlled drug* be used in the preliminary examination reports until a chemical examination can be conducted to determine the exact nature of the material.

II. DRUG ADDICTION AND ABUSE - IMPLICATIONS FOR THE CRIME SCENE INVESTIGATION

The following is not presented as a definitive or comprehensive discussion of drug addiction and abuse. However, there are some basic points concerning these matters that are critical for the crime scene investigator's knowledge concerning drugs.

The first such point concerns the question of what is meant by the term *addiction* and *abuse.* Addiction is primarily a matter of physical dependency of the user on the drug. When the addiction stage is reached, the user becomes sick if he is deprived of all he needs of the drug. Not all drugs have a physical dependence potential; however, most do. Some experts believe that in order for a person to become addicted to a drug (including alcohol) there must usually be some psychological maladjustment, and that individuals with such maladjustments need only to be introduced to and supplied with the drug for addiction to occur. As noted, some drugs, such as marihuana, are not physically addictive in the sense that the user will become ill if deprived of it. However, there are indications that any drug can induce a psychological dependency on the part of the user. Generally, a drug addict feels an overpowering desire or compulsion to continue taking the drug and to obtain it by any means. He has a tendency to increase the dose, because his body develops a tolerance for the drug that dampens the feeling of well-being he originally got from smaller doses of it.

Although there has been much research, and considerable speculation, on the various reasons people take drugs, a reliable general conclusion seems to be that drugs provide a means of quieting anxiety and shutting out problems. The important conclusion is that drug use in the modern society is not restricted to the "hippy," the young, the poor, or the racial minorities, - the classic stereotypes, but has a pervasive use pattern at all levels of the society.

The drug user today, perhaps more than at any other time, is in danger of poisoning by taking "street" drugs. A 2-year program of analysis and study at Midwest Research Institute of abused drugs acquired in the Kansas City Metropolitan Region turned up repeated instances of capsules or pills that had a completely different content than that represented by the pusher. Some contained poisonous substances which, if taken in sufficient quantity, could have lethal consequences. Ironically, some others contained no drug substances at all. Added to this danger of misrepresentation is the one of overdose, to which the addict, by virtue of his tendency to increase his dosages, is particularly vulnerable. Thus, an apparent deliberate poisoning, a homicide, an accidental death, or a suicide can all involve drug consumption.

Drug abuse, as a general term used here, applies to any use of a drug, whether or not legally possessed, to the extent that the user Has been or is likely to be adversely affected, (The terms *controlled* and *over-the-counter* or *non-controlled* are frequently used synonomous-ly with illegal and legal drugs, respectively.) Obviously, by that definition, even very low levels of the use of certain drugs by some people could qualify as abuse. In fact, as subsequent discussions will show, many drugs that have widely recognized medicinal value and are legally prescribed are also widely abused.

III. THE COMMONLY ABUSED DRUGS

Following are synopses of the various drugs or drug types that are often encountered by the police investigator, (Additional information concerning some of these types of drugs is presented in the table appearing at the end of this section,)

A. Heroin

This drug is a derivative of opium. It produces a "high" followed by a feeling of drowsiness and general well-being. It has a very high potential to create a physical dependency. It is usually taken by injecting it into the bloodstream, often using a modified eye dropper with a hypodermic needle attached as a syringe. Heroin can be sniffed; however, it has a very bitter taste, and is practically never taken orally unless encapsulated. Heroin is normally sold in "decks" and in clear gelatin capsules. For injection, the powder is dissolved in water, frequently in a bent teaspoon or metal bottle cap. The water is heated to boiling and the solution is then taken up through a cotton pledget into a needle and medical syringe or the type of modified eye dropper.

The common physical evidence associated with heroin use is the equipment needed to prepare the solution and make the injection, and the glassine bags, papers, capsules, or other containers that are used. In conducting a search, it is well to bear in mind some of the characteristic actions of heroin abusers in protecting their supply. The addict will go to extreme lengths to do this. Capsules or decks of heroin are sometimes placed inside toy balloons or condoms to enable the user to quickly swallow them if surprised, and later recover them from the feces. Women have been known to hide heroin decks in their vagina or in their undergarments. Some addicts have concealed heroin decks under the tongue or along the side of the mouth. All containers should be collected by the investigator. They should be marked and secured in such a way as to insure that no loss of contents will occur. The container and the collected materials are then placed in a clean envelope or paper bag, sealed, marked with the necessary information , and forwarded to the laboratory for identification.

Heroin is only one of the several drugs that falls in the general classification of the narcotics. Since narcotics have generally the same appearance, the field investigator will normally not be sure what kind of drug he has encountered or if it is a drug. This lack of knowledge will apply, more often than not, to any suspected drug substance. Therefore, until chemical tests are performed by the crime laboratory, it is a good policy to refer to known or suspected drug substances only as "controlled drugs." In a report, a notation such as "Four clear capsules containing a white crystalline powder" would meet technical and legal requirements. In all cases, it is important to state clearly the number and description of each item in the investigative notes and in the report.

B. Cocaine

Cocaine is also a narcotic drug, but it is obtained from the leaves of the coca bush rather than from the opium poppy. It is a white, odorless, fluffy, crystalline powder, and thus closely resembles hexoin in appearance. Also like heroin, it is commonly injected - sometimes sniffed. There are strong indications that a cocaine addict who has reached a high level of addiction (some inject the drug as many as 10 times a day) is incapable of planning a deliberate crime. However, if this is so, the addict may still commit crimes of violence out of imaginary fear of imminent danger. Some individuals experience intense excitation and a great sense of muscular strength under the influence of the drug.

The search for evidence items is the same as described for heroin.

C. Marihuana

Marihuana is a mixture of parts of the leaves and flowers of the hemp plant *Cannabis sativa*. Because this drug is today so prevalent and in such wide use, it is the most likely to be encountered, either in its dried form or as a live plant. Note the odd number of serrated blades having a common origin at the stem. There are usually five to seven blades to each leaf, but there may be as many as 21.

Material should be left in the container in which it was discovered. The material and the container are placed in a clean paper bag, sealed, and necessary information recorded on the outside of the bag. If possible, the original container of the drug should be marked before it is sealed in the bag.

Although marihuana may be eaten and the same effect attained, it is usually smoked. The cigarette sticks are usually rolled with two or three cigarette papers. Sometimes manufactured cigarettes are used by removing the tobacco filling and replacing it with marihuana. Various forms of pipes are also employed to smoke marihuana, ranging from the conventional tobacco pipe to hookahs, a form of water pipe. When burned, the drug gives off a sweet, pungent odor.

Marihuana has been known to be mixed with tobacco, catnip, dried leaves, and oregano. There have also been reports of deliberate "lacing" of the drug with addictive drugs such as heroin; however, this is definitely not a common practice.

The physical appearance of marihuana is sufficiently distinctive to allow an experienced investigator to identify it. Depending primarily on their state of dryness, the herbs are green to greenish brown in color, and usually hold some of the shape of the compression they were subjected to by the bulk processor (although this is not true of the "homegrown" supply). But even if identification of the drug seems fairly certain, it is good practice to describe it in the investigation records and reports only in terms of its physical appearance and approximate quantity.

Although marihuana usually has definite physical and psychological effects on the user, some persons experience nothing the first or second time they experiment with it; and many individuals have no manifestations that are discernible to others. Thus, the appearance of normality in a suspect does not exclude the possibility of fairly heavy and recent use of the drug.

The evidence to be collected in connection with this drug is the smoking apparatus, the drug itself, any residues and ashes resulting from smoking, particularly the contents of ash-trays, and paper and other containers that may have been used.

D. Hashish

Hashish is far more potent - and dangerous - to the user than is marihuana. It is in the form of a brown powder or is pressed into blocks or small pieces. It is frequently wrapped in small, tinfoil packets. However, it has been known to be mixed with instant coffee in an attempt to disguise it. Hashish may be either eaten or smoked -but it is usually the latter. Thus, the search is basically the same as for marihuana, allowing for the different bulk and appearance of the two drugs. While hashish is stronger than marihuana, its possession and sale still constitutes the offense of possession or sale of marihuana.

E. Hallucinogenic Drugs

These drugs, of which LSD, PCP and MDA are the most commonly abused, act on the central nervous system and on the psychic and mental functions. They produce visions, and dream-like thoughts -frequently very frightening. The user is usually unable to distinguish between fact and fantasy. LSD is available in most metropolitan areas in several forms - sometimes to the great detriment of the buyer who thinks he is getting something special. Foil packets, small tablets, small vials of liquid saturated sugar cubes or cookies, chewing gum, and capsules are relatively common forms of the drug's packaging. Foil is used to protect LSD from light, which reduces its strength. Foil should therefore be left intact when encountered.

Natural hallucinogens like mescaline and psilocybin are seldom encountered. The drugs purported to be mescaline and psilocybin are usually LSD and PCP.

Since all the hallucinogens are very powerful and can be absorbed through the skin, the investigator should not handle the material more than is absolutely necessary.

F. Barbiturates

These are a group of sedative and sleep-producing drugs that act on the central nervous system. They are usually taken orally, but

they can also be used intravenously or rectally. Because they are prescribed frequently by physicians, their presence on a crime scene does not automatically indicate criminal intent or wrong doing. However, it is well to note that this type of drug is the most often used means of committing nonviolent suicide. Most of the barbiturates are legally manufactured preparations, ranging from tablets, capsules, and suppositories to liquids. The best indication of abuse of these drugs is in the quantity of supply found. Abusers have been known to take as many as 40 barbiturate pills a day. The use of the barbiturates also often follows the excessive use of amphetamine drugs, which are discussed below, in order to "slow down." Therefore, amphetamines and barbiturates may be discovered together.

The use of alcohol before or along with the barbiturates may result in a "quick drunk" and possible death from respiratory failure. Both alcohol and barbiturates are depressants and their actions are addictive. Also, the barbiturates interfere with the body's normal disposition of alcohol.

Common types of barbiturate drugs are:
- Pentobarbital sodium
- Secobarbital sodium
- Amobarbital sodium with secobarbital sodium
- Amobarbital sodium
- Phenobarbital

G. Amphetamines

Contrary to the barbiturates, which are used medically to relax the central nervous system, amphetamines directly stimulate that system and produce excitation, alertness, and wakefulness. The degree of these effects depends on the dosage. They are commonly prescribed as an appetite depressant. Normally taken orally, amphetamines may also be injected. The drugs are produced in a wide variety of physical forms.

Because amphetamines are available only through prescription;, any such drugs collected should be left in the container they were found in, if any. The container should be processed for prints, the material examined as noted below; then sealed, marked and placed in a clean envelope or paper bag. This outer container should also be sealed and marked.

Amphetamines, or materials suspected to be such, that are not in a container should be suitably packaged, sealed, and marked.

Most amphetamines found will be of legal manufacture. There are a number of dosage forms - tablets and capsules being common. The investigator should note, and include in his report, the quantity, color, and shape of all tablets and capsules. If there are markings on tablets, those should be recorded exactly. If the appearance of the material inside the capsule can be determined without opening it, that information should be recorded as well.

As with all other suspected drug substances, the investigator should be cautious in making an identification based only on the physical appearance of the material. Prior to its analysis by the laboratory, it is always good practice to refer to the material in the notes and report in terms of its physical description and quantity.

Some examples of amphetamine drugs legally manufactured are:
- Amphetamine jsulfate
- Long-acting amphetamine sulfate capsules
- Dextroamphetamine sulfate

H. Methamphetamines

Methamphetamine (most commonly known as "speed") is chemically related to amphetamine but it has more central nervous system activity and correspondingly less effect on blood pressure and heart rate than amphetamine.

The abuse of methamphetamine is more widespread than ever before. Many abusers "shoot" (take intravenously) methamphetamine and eventually may build up to more than 100 times the medicinal dose. Thus, it is not surprising to discover these persons in an acute toxic state with death as a possible outcome. Methamphetamine for medical purposes is available on prescription only. It is available commercially under a variety of trade names. However, it is also manufactured in clandestine laboratories and is available in illicit channels as a crystalline powder in tablets, and in a variety of liquid forms.

I. Toxic Vapors

It has become relatively common practice among persons who experiment with drugs to intentionally smell or inhale the fumes of certain substances in the hope of achieving a condition of intoxication or euphoria (feeling of well-being or elation). Model airplane glue is a typical such substance used for "sniffing." However, inhaling fumes from gasoline, paint thinner, cabon tetrachloride, fingernail polish, acetone, and toluene will also produce forms of intoxication. The common practice is for the user to pour the substance into a plastic or paper bag, then place the bag tightly around the nose and mouth and inhale deeply. While such practice will usually produce only a blurring of vision, and other symptoms of intoxication, suffocation is always a distinct possibility as a result of the user breathing only vapors. If a death or serious injury has occured as a result of the deliberate inhalation of toxic vapors, there will usually be a distinct odor of the solvent about the person's clothing or on his breath, if he is still alive.

Evidence items to be searched for are plastic or paper bags with residues of the substance inhaled, rags or handkerchiefs containing dried material and, possibly, vomitus.

IV. IMPORTANT CAUTIONARY RULES IN COLLECTING DRUG SUBSTANCES

Some of the points summarized below have been made elsewhere in this section. However, because of their importance to the safety and health of the investigating officer, they bear repeating.

1. If an illicit laboratory operation is encountered and a scientist from the crime laboratory is not present, do not attempt to shut down the operation. Ventilate the area, call for assistance and wait outside. If an illicit laboratory operation is anticipated, include a member of the crime laboratory staff in the raid.
2. Never taste any material suspected of being a controlled drug.
3. Never smell materials suspected of containing controlled drugs.
4. Do not handle controlled drugs more than is absolutely necessary. After drugs have been handled, wash hands thoroughly as soon as possible.
5. Handle all chemical materials recovered with care. They may be highly flammable, caustic (burn the flesh) or susceptible to explosion.

6. Use particular care in searching a drug suspect, an automobile suspected of containing drugs or any area where it is possible that hypodermic syringes or makeshift needles may be hidden. Even slight pricks in the skin from such needles can be dangerous if the drug user has a communicable disease. Infectious hepatitis is common among persons who "shoot" drugs. If the skin is punctured, wash the area with soap and water and get medical attention.

V. THE USE OF FIELD KITS FOR IDENTIFICATION OF SUSPECTED DRUG SUBSTANCES

There are commercially available kits that allow police officers in the field to make presumptive tests of suspected drub substances. Such kits vary in degrees of reliability and the type drugs to which they are specific; however; detection of barbiturates, amphetamines, heroin, cocaine and marihuana are commonly within the detection range of the better ones.

The use of field testing devices to identify suspected drugs has the principal advantage to the police investigator of saving time. However, the disadvantages are the potential for error and the inability to detect a dangerous substance that is not within the range of the kit or procedure being used.

Virtually every crime laboratory in the United States has developed a primary capability in the identification of suspected drug^substances, with degrees of reliability in the analytical results that far exceed any that could be attained by use of field test kits. Therefore, the recommended procedure is to utilize the services of a laboratory for this purpose.

VI. INVESTIGATIONS

A. Identification of Drugs

A major portion of the illicit drug traffic involves heroin or marihuana. Heroin cannot be legally manufactured and is smuggled into the United States. Other dangerous drugs may be legally manufactured and their commercial appearances include pills, tablets, capsules, solution, infusions or tinctures of varying color and appearance.

It is not practical for the officer in the field, by physical examination, sniffing, tasting, etc., to attempt to determine whether a suspected substance is a dangerous drug. In addition, such attempts may be physically dangerous for the officer. They should be avoided.

In all cases, the only proper final determination of whether a suspected substance is a prohibited drug is analysis in the scientific laboratory.

Police officers have frequent occasion to search or "frisk" individuals or their cars, in connection with a crime or suspected crime not apparently connected with narcotics or dangerous drugs. On making the search or frisk the officer may find hypodermic syringes and/or needles or "the works." This is a slang term for a hypodermic syringe and needle or improvised means of injecting drugs, such as an eyedropper and a hypodermic needle, or even a razor blade or pin to open a vein and an eyedropper to inject the drug into the vein. A spoon or bottle cap used to heat or cook the heroin into solution is also part of "the works."

Opium pipes are large bowls fixed on top of a tube and mouthpiece, with a small opening in which the lit opium is put for smoking. Pipes for smoking "mary jane" or "pot" (marijuana) may be eastern style water pipes or hookahs, wherein the smoke is pulled through water for cooling, or regular tobacco pipes with the bowl much reduced in size by a wire screen or foil insertion, or pipes specially made for marijuana smoking with small metal bowls, possibly fashioned of a small pipe fitting or turned and bored from brass or even wood.

The items mentioned in the preceding two paragraphs are clear identifiers of the dangerous drug with which they are to be used. If residues of the drug are in or on them, they constitute thereby one element of a possession offense. In addition to such items, of course, the officer may find substances of various kinds which he suspects may be dangerous drugs.

B. Preliminary determination

The officer may make a preliminary determination that a ,suspected substance is or is not an illegal drug, on the basis of the following considerat ions:

1. Known character of the possessor
2. Admissions by the possessor
3. Refusal by the possessor to explain or identify the substance
4. Circumstances under which found
5. Concealed or hidden prior to finding (white tablets secreted in a trouser waistband or in a hollowed loaf of bread or a shoe heel are more likely to be a narcotic than to be aspirin)
6. Information from an informant
7. Physical appearance (a white powder in a clear plastic envelope or fold could be heroin; a hand-rolled cigarette whose contents do not look like the usual tobacco could be a "reefer" of marihuana
8. Examination by trade experts (experienced pharmacists or expert personnel of drug supply and chemical firms may be able to recognize that substances are dangerous

drugs, in case of commercial preparations and tablets, by shape, appearance and markings)

9. Pharmacists can make on-the-spot chemical tests for identification of some narcotics. Such examination should always be supplemented by formal scientific laboratory analysis

10. Packaging-dangerous drugs may occasionally be found in an original commercial bottle or package, showing identification of the substances contained, such as "Demerol," "Morphine Sulfate 1/4 Grain," "Codeine," etc.)

11. Field testing, in case of some dangerous drugs, with a prepared kit. (The Federal Bureau of Narcotics and Dangerous Drugs utilizes such field kits. In some instances such kits may be made available to local officers on request to this Bureau.)

C. Searches

The main problem in a search for dangerous drugs is usually the small size of the object sought - it may be concealed in pants cuffs, hat bands, clothing seams, in body openings, cigarette packages, a pen, a letter, a book, paper, etc. Searches must be very detailed. Consideration should be given to having a physician search body openings when available information is that the subject is in fact in possession of narcotics, and other searching fails to discover them. Subjects must be isolated during search, to prevent their concealing the narcotics in the upholstery of a chair, etc.

In searching automobiles, the search must be extremely detailed, including putting the car on a lift, and carefully examining its underside. Hub caps and spare tires should always be suspect, as well as the upholstery. Officers should be alert for special hiding places welded on the underside of fenders, frame members, etc., and for "traps" with spring-loaded or other openings concealed in which dangerous drugs may be hidden from casual search.

In buildings, places suspect as hiding places for dangerous drugs would be electric outlets and light fixtures, behind trim, in crevices and breaks of walls, and, of course, all usual hiding places such as cabinets, chests, closets, joists, water tanks of toilets and containers of food, cosmetics, etc. In cities and towns, one favored device has been to suspend narcotics by a cord from a windowsill, the pressure of the lower window sash holding the cord. When the window is opened for search, the narcotic falls to the ground and may well be overlooked by the searcher.

D. Users and Addicts

A heroin or opiate user, who has had a normal "shot" or "fix" appears calm and relaxed, but it will be found that his eye pupils have contracted considerably and do not react normally to light -he may have a fixed stare. The user who is in need of a "shot" will be restless, nervous, anxious. He will probably yawn frequently, have runny eyes and nose, and sweat more than usual. His eye pupils may be enlarged, his muscles will twitch, and the skin may show "goose-flesh. " Other symptoms are severe aches, vomiting, diarrhea, sleeplessness, a rise in temperature and blood pressure, and an increased breathing rate.

The heroin user will have needle puncture marks, scabs, and,possibly, sores or even ulcers from old punctures, The marks are more usually on the forearm but may be on any other part of the body, including the hands.

Marihuana may be eaten or smoked. It affects the higher nerve centers and is first manifested by a curious delirium, accompanied by exaltation of imaginative functions and not infrequently by hallucinations, followed by a remarkable loss of the sense of time. In a general way, the marihuana user under its influence has a euphoria like one intoxicated on alcohol. He loses inhibitions, in addition. He may have some reddening of the eyes and/or a flushed complexion.

Barbiturates are likely to produce symptoms similar to drunkenness, such as slurring of speech, lack of balance, and a quick temper. Serious misuse of barbiturates can result in very dangerous withdrawal problems, including comvulsions, and possibly death.

When a suspected addict or drug user is taken into custody, officers should be alert to summon medical assistance and to have the subject examined by a physician. In addition, certain illnesses may counterfeit the appearance of drug addiction, and lack of medical attention could result in death or severe damage to an innocent subject's physical well-being.

E. Patrol

The officer on patrol should be continually alert for signs of possible dangerous drug sales or use. Low-class candy stores, luncheonettes, billiard parlors and similar establishments where there appears to be constant activity, corner hangouts of male and female adolescents, rooming houses where there is an unusual number of people going in and out, people on the street who seem to be frequently in businesslike conversation with a number of other people, schools where older boys and men hang around, well dressed or "sharp" individuals who loiter around and seem to have no employment, are some of the things to be given special attention.

Attention should be given to roofs, cellars, stairways, hallways and vacant premises where persons have been known to congregate and use marihuana or other narcotics. Such spots may sometimes be identified by finding empty gelatin capsules or small papers in which narcotics may have been folded, medicine droppers, bent safety pins, numerous burnt matches, bent spoons or bottle caps showing signs of having been used to "cook" or heat water for dissolving heroin for a "shot," and pieces of cotton used to strain the cooked "shot."

When any observation is made indicating possible dangerous drug activity, arrangements should be made for continued observation. The uniformed officer is at a considerable disadvantage in this regard and plainclothes officers must ordinarily be used. Discreet surveillance will generally be required to develop enough information to warrant arrest. The main objective of the officer should be to develop facts giving reasonable grounds to seek issuance of search warrants, arrest warrants or for summary arrest.

Careful observation should be made of the automobiles of likely suspects. It will frequently be found that users of "reefers" are not neat and cars will have flakes of marihuana scattered on the floors, the butt ends of reefers carelessly stamped out, cigarette papers fallen or discarded, open or crumpled, all indicators of possible marihuana use.

F. Sellers or Peddlers

It is common practice for those who sell narcotics to the ultimate user to: (1) carry small amounts (to avoid prosecution as a seller instead of as a mere possessor if arrested), (2) make contact with the buyer without carrying narcotics (to avoid evidence if contact is observed and arrest made), (3) make delivery to buyer by previously hiding the narcotic and informing the buyer of the hiding place.

Some sellers will carry the narcotic with them in a crumpled cigarette package and drop it on the street near the customer after transacting the sale. Some may have a girl friend accompanying them who will carry the narcotic on or in her body and when the sale is transacted, will go to a woman's toilet, remove the amount needed and deliver it to the user. Various other devices of a similar nature will be used.

G. Personal Danger

Officers must bear in mind that dangerous drug and particularly narcotics users are frequently in an abnormal condition. Due caution must be used in narcotics cases at all times, in respect to arrests.

The dangerous drug traffic involves large sums of money and enormous profits and the professionals engaged in smuggling, distributing and supplying do not hesitate to commit murder to silence witnesses, avoid loss of expensive merchandise or evade capture. Officers must use care and discretion not only for their personal safety but for the safety of witnesses, informants and others involved in a case.

E. Informants

A basic ingredient of a successful dangerous drug enforcement program is informants. Every effort should be made to develop informants or sources of information not only among addicts and others connected with the narcotics trade, but among non-users in a position to make pertinent observations or otherwise learn of information pertinent to the trade, particularly as to individual sales to users.

When dealing with informants, officers must use the greatest care to avoid the informant deliberately or carelessly Msetting up" a subject by means of entrapment. It is entrapment where the methods used to obtain the evidence are such as to create a substantial risk that the offense will be committed by a person not otherwise disposed to commit it (P.L. Sec. 35.40).

I. Radio in Possession

If an offender or suspect is found in possession of a radio capable of receiving police frequencies, or a walkie-talkie or similar device, refer to special information in this area.

VII. DRUGS (CONTROLLED SUBSTANCES)

Effective September 1, 1973, the Penal Law drug offenses changed to "controlled substance" offenses. This terminology, and the drugs, chemicals, or materials included as "controlled substances" conform to the Public Health Law and to the Federal law on narcotic and other controlled drugs. Federal law uses similar schedules.

A. Controlled Substance

A "controlled substance" under the Penal Law is any substance listed in Schedules I, II, III, IV, or V of Public Health Law Section 3306 (P.L. Sec, 220.00, subd. 5),

B. Penal Law Classifications of Controlled Substances

The Penal Law applies different penalties, of varied severity, to possession, possession with intent to sell, and selling of different classifications of controlled substances. The penalties depend not only on the classification of the controlled substance but also on the quantity involved.

The quantities necessary to constitute each particular classification of offense are set out under the headings, "Crimes OF CRIMINAL POSSESSION OF A CONTROLLED SUBSTANCE" and "CRIMES OF CRIMINAL SALE OF A CONTROLLED SUBSTANCE."

The Penal Law's classifications of kinds of controlled substances are as follows:

1. DANGEROUS DEPRESSANT: Any controlled substance listed in Schedule II (d), III (a) (1) or IV (a) (P.L. Sec. 220.00, subd. 12).

2. DEPRESSANT: Any controlled substance listed in Schedule IV (b) (P.L, Sec. 220.00, subd. 13).

3. HALLUCINOGEN; Any controlled substance lised in Schedule I (c) 7, 13, 14, 15, 16, and 17 (P,L. Sec. 220,00, subd. 9),

4. HALLUCINOGENIC SUBSTANCE: Any controlled substance listed in Schedule I (c) except concentrated cannabis, lysergic acid diethylamide or a hallucinogen (i,e,, only items in Schedule I (c) 1, 2, 3, 4, 5,

6, 8, 11,.and 12) (P.L. Sec, 220.00, subd. 10),

5. LSD (Lysergic acid diethylamide): This drug is named in various penal sections on possession and sale; it is listed in Schedule I (c) as item 9.

6. MARIJUANA: Marijuana or concentrated cannabis, as those terms are defined in Section 3302 of the Public Health Law (P.L. Sec. 220.00, subd. 6).

a. Marijuana means: all parts of the plant of the genus Cannabis, whether growing or not; the seeds thereof; the resin extracted from any part of the plant; and every compound, manufacture, salt, derivative, mixture, or preparation of the plant, its seeds or resin. It does not include the mature stalks of the plant, fiber produced from the stalks, oil, or cake made from the seeds of the plant, any other compound, manufacture, salt, derivative, mixture, or preparation of the mature stalks (except the resin extracted therefrom), fiber, oil, or cake, or the sterilized seed of the plant which is incapable of germination CPubl. H. L, Sec, 3302, subd. 20).

b. Concentrated cannabis means:

(1) the separated resin, whether crude or purified, obtained from a plant of the genus Cannabis; or

(2) a material, preparation, mixture, compound or other substance which contains more than two and one-half percent by weight of delta-9 tetrahydrocannabinol, or its isomer, delta-8 dibenzopyran numbering system, or delta-1 tetrahydrocannabinol or its isomer, delta 1 (b) monoterpene numbering system (Publ. H. L. Sec. 3302, subd. 5).

7. METHAMPHETAMINE: This drug is named in various penal law sections on possession and sale; it is listed in Schedule II (c) as item 3.

8. NARCOTIC DRUG: Any controlled substance listed in Schedule I (a), I (b), II (a) or II (b) (P.L. Sec. 220.00, subd. 7).

9. NARCOTIC PREPARATION: Any controlled substance listed in Schedule III (b) or III (c) (P.L. Sec. 220.00, subd. 8).

10. STIMULANT: Any controlled substance listed in Schedule II (c) (P.L. Sec. 220.00, subd. 11).

11. OTHER CONTROLLED SUBSTANCES: The only controlled substances which are not listed as a Dangerous Depressant, Depressant, Hallugino-gen, Hallucinogenic Substances, LSD, Marijuana, Methamphetamine, Narcotic Drug, Narcotic Preparation or Stimulant are those controlled substances in Schedule III (a) 2 through 10 and V, 1 through 5.

C. Controlled Substance Offenses Generally

The Penal Law crimes in respect to the various classifications of "controlled substances" all involve either an unlawful possession or an unlawful sale.

The Penal Law specifically defines "unlawful" to mean in violation of Article 33 of the Public Health Law. That article permits possession or sale of controlled substances only in accordance with strict rules as to licenses to manufacture and distribute, prescriptions, etc. It completely forbids either the manufacture or possession of some controlled substances, such as LSD and heroin, except for limited scientific purposes.

The Penal Law defines the word "sell" to mean sell, exchange, give, or dispose of to another, or to offer or agree to sell, exchange, give, or dispose of to another (P.L. Sec. 220.00, subd. 1).

D. Crimes of "Criminal Possession of a Controlled Substance"

The various degrees of Criminal Possession of a Controlled Substance and their crime classifications are as follows:

1. SEVENTH DEGREE (P.L. Sec. 220.03 - Class A Misdemeanor
2. SIXTH DEGREE (P.L. Sec. 220.06) - Class D Felony
3. FIFTH DEGREE (P.L. Sec. 220.09) - Class C Felony
4. FOURTH DEGREE (P.L. Sec. 220.12) - Class B Felony
5. THIRD DEGREE (P.L. Sec. 220.16) - Class A-III Felony
6. SECOND DEGREE (P.L. Sec. 220.18) - Class A-II Felony
7. FIRST DEGREE (P.L. Sec. 220.21) - Class A-I Felony

E. Crimes of "Criminal Sale of a Controlled Substance"

The various degrees of Criminal Sale of a Controlled Substance and their crime classifications are as follows:

1. SIXTH DEGREE (P.L. Sec. 220.31) - Class D Felony
2. FIFTH DEGREE (P.L. Sec. 220.34) - Class C Felony
3. FOURTH DEGREE (P.L. Sec. 220.37) - Class B Felony
4. THIRD DEGREE (P.L. Sec. 220.39) - Class A-III Felony
5. SECOND DEGREE (P.L. Sec. 220.41) - Class A-II Felony
6. FIRST DEGREE (P.L. Sec. 220.43) - Class A-I Felony

———

VIII. POLICE OFFICER'S GUIDE TO CERTAIN ABUSED DRUGS

Name	Some Street Names	Chemical or Trade Name	How Taken	Dependence Potential
Heroin	H., Horse, Scat, Smack, Junk, Snow, Harry, Joy Powder	Diacetyl-morphine (Depressant)	Injected Sniffed	Physical and psychic
Morphine	White stuff, Miss Emma, M., Dreamer	Morphine Sulfate (Depressant)	Swallowed Injected	Physical and psychic
Codeine	Schoolboy	Methyl-morphine (Depressant)	Swallowed	Physical and psychic
Marihuana	Pot, Grass, Locoweed, Mary Jane, Hashish, Tea, Indian Hay, Giggle Weed, Giggle-smoke	Cannabis Sativa (Stimulant, depressant or hallucinogen, depending on user)	Smoked Swallowed (Hashish, the concentrated form, may be sniffed)	No physical dependency; possible psychic
Cocaine	Speed Balls, Gold Dust, Coke, The Leaf, Snow, Star Dust	Methylester of benzoyl-ecgonine (Stimulant)	Sniffed Injected Swallowed	Psychic
Amphetamines	Bennies, Dexies, Co-Pilots, Wake-ups, Footballs, Hearts, Pep Pills, Speed	Benzedrine, Preludin, Dexedrine, Methedrine, Dexoxyn (Stimulants)	Swallowed Injected	Psychic only
Barbiturates	Red Birds, Yellow Jackets, Dandy, Phennies, Peanuts, Blue Heavens	Phenobarbital, Nembutal, Seconal, Amytal (Depressants)	Swallowed Injected	Physical and psychic
Hallucinogens (LSD and DMT)	LSD, Acid, Sugar, Big D, Cubes, Trips, etc. DMT - Businessman's High	d-lysergic acid diethylamide (LSD) Dimethyl-tryptamine (DMT) (Hallucinogens)	Swallowed (LSD) Injected (DMT)	No physical dependency Psychic dependency uncertain
Mescaline	Cactus, Peyote	3,4,5-tri-methoxy-phenethyla-mine (Hallucinogen)	Swallowed	No physical dependency Psychic dependency uncertain

POLICE OFFICER'S GUIDE TO CERTAIN ABUSED DRUGS
(Continued)

	Primary Effect on Users	Symptoms That Help Identify Users	Some Dangers of Abuse
Heroin	Generally sedative-rarely does it excite. Initial reaction may be unpleasant; but soon subsides to drowsiness and feeling of well-being.	Slow pulse and respiration. User is drowsy, very calm in demeanor when under the influence of the drug. Loss of appetite. Overdose may produce convulsions. Pupils of eyes constricted.	High rate of dependence. Must increase dose to obtain the desired effect. Drastic withdrawal symptoms. Because the drug is a respiratory depressant, can cause coma and death. User has no ability or desire to do constructive work. When deprived of the drug, becomes extremely agitated and uncomfortable.
Morphine	Heroin-like	Like heroin, but somewhat slower to act.	Like heroin, except that dependence may develop somewhat slower.
Codeine	Deadens pain and is a cough suppressant. Very little of the feeling of well-being produced by heroin and morphine.	Large doses, taken intravenously, are required to produce manifestations of effects similar to heroin and morphine. Usually not much evidence of effect from oral dosage.	Can be addictive; however, only when taken in large amounts. For obvious reasons, seldom used by hardened addicts, except to tide over during periods when heroin or morphine are not available.
Marihuana	Initial use may produce no particular effect; later feeling of great perceptiveness, distortion of time and space, possibly erratic behavior, unwarranted hilarity, feeling of great pleasure.	Exhilarated, talkative, but may only sit and stare. Exaggerated sense of ability is common. May experience and verbalize "visions." The effect is personality dependent to a great degree. Thus, very difficult to generalize.	May lose normal restraint and reserves, thus, attempt acts that are dangerous. Seldom produces aggressive behavior. A psychic dependence is possible.
Cocaine	Oral doses can relieve hunger and fatigue. Intravenous doses can cause great excitability and manical behavior; hallucinations.	Manical behavior, hallucinations, muscular twitching, possibly convulsions. Pupils are dilated, and the individual is generally hyperactive.	Paranoia, possibly convulsions, and death from an overdose. There is a very strong psychic dependency potential with this drug, but apparently no physical dependency.

POLICE OFFICER'S GUIDE TO CERTAIN ABUSED DRUGS
(Continued)

	Primary Effect on Users	Symptoms That Help Identify Users	Some Dangers of Abuse
Amphetamines	Normal dose can produce a wakeful attitude, increased alertness, and initiative.	If the user has taken an intravenous dose, may exhibit cocaine-like effects (manical behavior). May exhibit an unusual degree of "nerve."	Because of the lessened sense of personal danger, the drug may cause the user to become dangerous to himself and others. Prolonged excessive use can cause erratic and aggressive behavior.
Barbiturates	Small doses serve to relax, make good humored. With dose progression, the individual becomes sluggish and sedated.	Abuse of the drug will produce behavior that is very much like alcohol drunkenness. Such behavior, in the absence of the odor of alcohol, is strong indication of barbiturate use.	Coma and death from respiratory failure. Convulsions and severe withdrawal symptoms also probable with abuse. Very hazardous when taken with alcohol.
Hallucinogens	Hallucinations are almost invariably produced. Depression, exhilaration, serious mental changes common.	Complete personality changes are possible. May "see" smells and "hear" tastes. Generally irrational behavior and verbalizing.	Permanent mental derangement is always a danger. Individuals perceive false ability (to fly, for example) and thus may commit dangerous acts. Possibility of recurrence of hallucinations or psychotoxic episodes weeks after taking the drug.
Mescaline	Produces a feeling of exhilaration in many users. Others experience anxiety.	As noted at left. In addition, the individual may complain of gastric distress.	The long-term effects of heavy use are uncertain.

—

DRUG ABUSE

CONTENTS

DRUG ABUSE
CONTROLLED SUBSTANCES ACT

The Controlled Substances Act (CSA), Title II of the Comprehensive Drug Abuse Prevention and Control Act of 1970, is the legal foundation of the government's fight against abuse of drugs and other substances. This law is a consolidation of numerous laws regulating the manufacture and distribution of narcotics, stimulants, depressants, hallucinogens, anabolic steroids and chemicals used in the illicit production of controlled substances.

CONTROLLING DRUGS OR OTHER SUBSTANCES

FORMAL SCHEDULING

The CSA places all substances which were in some manner regulated under existing Federal law into one of five schedules. This placement is based upon the substance's medical use, potential for abuse, and safety or dependence liability. The Act also provides a mechanism for substances to be controlled, or added to a schedule; decontrolled, or removed from control; and rescheduled or transferred from one schedule to another. The procedure for these actions is found in Section 201 of the Act (21 D.S.C. 811).

Proceedings to add, delete, or change the schedule of a drug or other substance may be initiated by the Drug Enforcement Administration (DEA), the Department of Health and Human Services (HHS), or by petition from any interested party: the manufacturer of a drug, a medical society or association, a pharmacy association, a public interest group concerned with drug abuse, a state or local government agency, or an individual citizen. When a petition is received by DEA, the agency begins its own investigation of the drug.

The agency also may begin an investigation of a drug at any time based upon information received from law enforcement laboratories, state and local law enforcement and regulatory agencies, or other sources of information.

Once DEA has collected the necessary data, the Administrator of DEA, by authority of the Attorney General, requests from HHS a scientific and medical evaluation and recommendation as to whether the drug or other substance should be controlled or removed from control. This request is sent to the Assistant Secretary of Health of HHS. HHS solicits information from the Commissioner of the Food and Drug Administration (FDA), evaluations and recommendations from the National Institute on Drug Abuse, and on occasion from the scientific and medical community at large. The Assistant Secretary, by authority of the Secretary, compiles the information and transmits back to DEA a medical and scientific evaluation regarding the drug or other substance, a recommendation as to whether the drug should be controlled, and in what schedule it should be placed.

The medical and scientific evaluations are binding on DEA with respect to scientific and medical matters. The recommendation on scheduling is binding only to the extent that if HHS recommends that the substance not be controlled, DEA may not control the substance.

Once DEA has received the scientific and medical evaluation from HHS, the Administrator will evaluate all available data and make a final decision whether to propose that a drug or other substance should be controlled and into which schedule it should be placed.

The threshold issue is whether the drug or other substance has potential for abuse. If a drug does not have a potential for abuse, it cannot be controlled. Although the term "potential for abuse" is not defined in the CSA, there is much discussion of the term in the legislative history of the Act. The following items are indicators that a drug or other substance has a potential for abuse:

1) There is evidence that individuals are taking the drug or other substance in amounts sufficient to create a hazard to their health or to the safety of other individuals or to the community; or

2) There is significant diversion of the drug or other substance from legitimate drug channels; or

3) Individuals are taking the drug or other substance on their own initiative rather than on the basis of medical advice from a practitioner licensed by law to administer such drugs; or

4) The drug is a new drug so related in its action to a drug or other substance already listed as having a potential for abuse to make it likely that the drug will have the same potential for abuse as such drugs, thus making it reasonable to assume that there may be significant diversions from legitimate channels, significant use contrary to or without medical advice, or that it has a substantial capability of creating hazards to the health of the user or to the safety of the community. Of course, evidence of actual abuse of a substance is indicative that a drug has a potential for abuse.

In determining into which schedule a drug or other substance should be placed, or whether a substance should be decontrolled or rescheduled, certain factors are required to be considered. Specific findings are not required for each factor. These factors are listed in Section 201 (c), [21 U.S.C. 811 (c)], of the CSA and are as follows:

1) *The drug's actual or relative potential for abuse.*

2) *Scientific evidence of the drug's pharmacological effects.* The state of know 1edge with respect to the effects of a specific drug is, of course, a major consideration. For example, it is vital to know whether or not a drug has a hallucinogenic effect if it is to be controlled because of that. The best available knowledge of the pharmacological properties of a drug should be considered.

3) *The state of current scientific knowledge regarding the substance.* Criteria (2) and (3) are closely related. However, (2) is primarily concerned with pharmacological effects and (3) deals with all scientific knowledge with respect to the substance.

4) *Its history and current pattern of abuse.* To determine whether or not a drug should be controlled, it is important to know the pattern of abuse of that substance, including the socio-economic characteristics of the segments of the population involved in such abuse.

5) *The scope, duration, and significance of abuse.* In evaluating existing abuse, the Administrator must know not only the pattern of abuse but whether the abuse is widespread. In reaching his decision, the Administrator should consider the economics of regulation and enforcement attendant to such a decision. In addition, he should be aware of the social significance and impact of such a decision upon those people, especially the young that would be affected by it.

6) *What, if any, risk there is to the public health.* If a drug creates dangers to the public health, in addition to or because of its abuse potential, then these dangers must also be considered by the Administrator.

7) *The drug's psychic or physiological dependence liability.* There must be an assessment of the extent to which a drug is physically addictive or psychologically habit-forming, if such information is known.

8) *Whether the substance is an immediate precursor of a substance already controlled.* The CSA allows inclusion of immediate precursors on this basis alone into the appropriate schedule and thus safeguards against possibilities of clandestine manufacture.

After considering the above listed factors, the Administrator must make specific findings concerning the drug or other substance. This will determine into which schedule the drug or other substance will be placed. These schedules are established by the CSA. They are as follows:

Schedule I

- The drug or other substance has a high potential for abuse.
- The drug or other substance has no currently accepted medical use in treatment in the United States.
- There is a lack of accepted safety for use of the drug or other substance under medical supervision.
- Some Schedule I substances are heroin, LSD, marijuana, and methamphetamine

Schedule II

- The drug or other substance has a high potential for abuse.
- The drug or other substance has a currently accepted medical use in treatment in the United States or a currently accepted medical use with severe restrictions.
- Abuse of the drug or other substance may lead to severe psychological or physical dependence.
- Schedule II substances include morphine, PCP, cocaine, methadone, and methamphetamine.

Schedule III

- The drug or other substance has a potential for abuse less than the drugs or other substances in Schedules I and II.
- The drug or other substance has a currently accepted medical use in treatment in the United States.
- Abuse of the drug or other substance may lead to moderate or low physical dependence or high psychological dependence.
- Anabolic steroids, codeine and hydrocodone with aspirin or Tylenol®, and some barbiturates are Schedule III substances.

Schedule IV

- The drug or other substance has a low potential for abuse relative to the drugs or other substances in Schedule III.
- The drug or other substance has a currently accepted medical use in treatment in the United States.
- Abuse of the drug or other substance may lead to limited physical dependence or psychological dependence relative to the drugs or other substances in Schedule III.
- Included in Schedule IV are Darvon®, Talwin®, Equanil®, Valium® and Xanax®.

Schedule V

> The drug or other substance has a low potential for abuse relative to the drugs or other substances in Schedule IV.
> The drug or other substance has a currently accepted medical use in treatment in the United States.
> Abuse of the drug or other substances may lead to limited physical dependence or psychological dependence relative to the drugs or other substances in Schedule IV.
> Over-the-counter cough medicines with codeine are classified in Schedule V.

When the Administrator of DEA has determined that a drug or other substance should be controlled, decontrolled, or rescheduled, a proposal to take action is published in the F federal Register. The proposal invites all interested persons to file comments with DEA. Affected parties may also request a hearing with DEA. If no hearing is requested, DEA will evaluate all comments received and publish a final order in the Federal Register, controlling the drug as proposed or with modifications based upon the written comments filed. This order will set the effective dates for imposing the various requirements imposed under the CSA.

If a hearing is requested, DEA will enter into discussions with the party or parties requesting a hearing in an attempt to narrow the issue for litigation. If necessary, a hearing will then be held before an Administrative Law Judge. The judge will take evidence on factual issues and hear arguments on legal questions regarding the control of the drug. Depending on the scope and complexity of the issues, the hearing may be brief or quite extensive. The Administrative Law Judge, at the close of the hearing, prepares findings of fact and conclusions of law and a recommended decision which is submitted to the Administrator of DEA. The Administrator will review these documents, as well as the underlying material, and prepare his/her own findings of fact and conclusions of law (which may or may not be the same as those drafted by the Administrative Law Judge). The Administrator then publishes a final order in the Federal Register either scheduling the drug or other substance or declining to do so.

Once the final order is published in the *Federal Register*, interested parties have 30 days to appeal to a U.S. Court of Appeals to challenge the order. Findings of fact by the Administrator are deemed conclusive if supported by "substantial evidence." The order imposing controls is not stayed during the appeal, however, unless so ordered by the Court.

Emergency or Temporary Scheduling

The CSA was amended by the Comprehensive Crime Control Act of 1984. This Act included a provision which allows the Administrator of DE A to place a substance, on a temporary basis, into Schedule I when necessary to avoid an imminent hazard to the public safety.

This emergency scheduling authority permits the scheduling of a substance which is not currently controlled, is being abused, and is a risk to the public health while the formal rule making procedures described in the CSA are being conducted. This emergency scheduling applies only to substances with no accepted medical use. A temporary scheduling order may be issued for one year with a possible extension of up to six months if formal scheduling procedures have been initiated. The proposal and order are published in the Federal Register as are the proposals and orders for formal scheduling. [21 V.S.C. 811 (1)]

Controlled Substance Analogues

A new class of substances was created by the Anti-Drug Abuse Act of 1986. Controlled substance analogues are substances which are not controlled substances, but may be found in the illicit traffic. They are structurally or pharmacologically similar to Schedule I or II controlled substances and have no legitimate medical use. A substance which meets the definition of a controlled substance analogue and is intended for human consumption is treated under the CSA as if it were a controlled substance in Schedule I.

International Treaty Obligations

U. S. treaty obligations may require that a drug or other substance be controlled under the CSA, or rescheduled if existing controls are less stringent than those required by a treaty. The procedures for these scheduling actions are found in Section 201 (d) of the Act. [21 V.S.C. 811 (d)]

The United States is a party to the Single Convention on Narcotic Drugs of 1961, designed to establish effective control over international and domestic traffic in narcotics, coca leaf, cocaine, and cannabis. A second treaty, the Convention on Psychotropic Sub- stances of 1971, which entered into force in 1976, is designed to establish comparable control over stimulants, depressants, and hallucinogens. Congress ratified this treaty in 1980.

II. REGULATION

The CSA creates a closed system of distribution for those authorized to handle controlled substances. The cornerstone of this system is the registration of all those authorized by DEA to handle controlled substances. All individuals and firms that are registered are required to maintain complete and accurate inventories and records of all transactions involving controlled substances, as well as security for the storage of controlled substances.

Registration

Any person who handles or intends to handle controlled substances must obtain a registration issued by DEA. A unique number is assigned to each legitimate handler of controlled drugs: importer, exporter, manufacturer, distributor, hospital, pharmacy, practitioner, and researcher. This number must be made available to the supplier by the customer prior to the purchase of a controlled substance. Thus, the opportunity for unauthorized transactions is greatly diminished.

Recordkeeping

The CSA requires that complete and accurate records be kept of all quantities of controlled substances manufactured, purchased, and sold. Each substance must be inventoried every two years. Some limited exceptions to the recordkeeping requirements may apply to certain categories of registrants.

From these records it is possible to trace the flow of any drug from the time it is first imported or manufactured through the distribution level, to the pharmacy or hospital that dispensed it, and then to the actual patient who received the drug. The mere existence of this requirement is sufficient to discourage many forms of diversion. It actually serves large drug corporations as an internal check to uncover diversion, such as pilferage by employees.

There is one distinction between scheduled items for recordkeeping requirements. Records for Schedule I and II drugs must be kept separate from all other records of the handler; records for Schedule III, IV, and V substances must be kept in a "readily retrievable" form. The former method allows for more expeditious investigations involving the highly abusable substances in Schedules I and II.

Distribution

The keeping of records is required for distribution of a controlled substance from one manufacturer to another, from manufacturer to distributor, and from distributor to dispenser. In the case of Schedule I and II drugs, the supplier must have a special order form from the customer. This order form (DEA Form 222) is issued by DEA only to persons who are properly registered to handle Schedules I and II. The form is preprinted with the name and address of the customer. The drugs must be shipped to this name and address. The use of this device is a special reinforcement of the registration requirement; it makes doubly certain that only authorized individuals may obtain Schedule I and II drugs. Another benefit of the form is the special monitoring it permits. The form is issued in triplicate: the customer keeps one copy; two copies go to the supplier who, after filling the order, keeps a copy and forwards the third copy to the nearest DEA office.

For drugs in Schedules III, IV, and V, no order form is necessary. The supplier in each case, however, is under an obligation to verify the authenticity of the customer. The supplier is held fully accountable for any drugs which are shipped to a purchaser who does not have a valid registration.

Manufacturers must submit periodic reports of the Schedule I and II controlled substances they produce in bulk and dosage forms. They also report the manufactured quantity and form of each narcotic substance listed in Schedules III, IV, and V, as well as the quantity of synthesized psychotropic substances listed in Schedules I, II, III, and IV. Distributors of controlled substances must report the quantity and form of all their transactions of controlled drugs listed in Schedules I and II and narcotics listed in Schedule III. Both manufacturers and distributors are required to provide reports of their annual inventories of these controlled substances. This data is entered into a system called the Automated Reports and Consolidated Orders System (ARCOS). It enables DEA to monitor the distribution of controlled substances throughout the country, and to identify retail level registrants that receive unusual quantities of controlled substances.

Dispensing to Patients

The dispensing of a controlled substance is the delivery of the controlled substance to the ultimate user, who may be a patient or research subject. Special control mechanisms operate here as well. Schedule I drugs are those which have no currently accepted medical use in the United States; they may, therefore, be used in the United States only in research situations. They generally are supplied by only a limited number of firms to properly registered and qualified researchers. Controlled substances may be dispensed by a practitioner by direct administration, by prescription, or by dispensing from office supplies. Records must be maintained by the practitioner of all dispensing of controlled substances from office supplies and of certain administrations. The CSA does not require the practitioner to maintain copies of prescriptions, but certain states require the use of multiple copy prescriptions for Schedule II and other specified controlled substances.

The determination to place drugs on prescription is within the jurisdiction of the FDA. Unlike other prescription drugs, however, controlled substances are subject to additional restrictions. Schedule II prescription orders must be written and signed by the practitioner; they may not be telephoned into the pharmacy except in an emergency. In addition, a prescription for a Schedule II drug may not be refilled; the patient must see the practitioner again in order to obtain more drugs. For Schedule III and IV drugs, the prescription order may be either written or oral (that is, by telephone to the pharmacy). In addition, the patient may (if authorized by the practitioner) have the prescription refilled up to five times and at any time within six months from the date of the initial dispensing.

Schedule V includes some prescription drugs and many over-the-counter narcotic preparations, including antitussives and antidiarrheal. Even here, however, the law imposes restrictions beyond those normally required for the over-the-counter sales; for example, the patient must be at least 18 years of age, must offer some form of identification, and have his or her name entered into a special log maintained by the pharmacist as part of a special record.

Quotas

DEA limits the quantity of Schedule I and II controlled substances which may be produced in the United States in any given calendar year. By utilizing available data on sales and inventories of these controlled substances, and taking into account estimates of drug usage provided by the FDA, DEA establishes annual aggregate production quotas for Schedule I and II controlled substances. The aggregate production quota is allocated among the various manufacturers who are registered to manufacture the specific drug. DEA also allocates the amount of bulk drug which may be procured by those companies which prepare the drug into dosage units.

Security

DEA registrants are required by regulation to maintain certain security for the storage and distribution of controlled substances. Manufacturers and distributors of Schedule I and II substances must store controlled substances in specially constructed vaults or highly rated safes, and maintain electronic security for all storage areas. Lesser physical security requirements apply to retail level registrants such as hospitals and pharmacies.

All registrants are required to make every effort to ensure that controlled substances in their possession are not diverted into the illicit market. This requires operational as well as physical security. For example, registrants are responsible for ensuring that controlled substances are distributed only to other registrants that are authorized to receive them or to legitimate patients and consumers.

III. PENALTIES

The CSA provides penalties for unlawful manufacturing, distribution, and dispensing of controlled substances. The penalties are basically determined by the schedule of the drug or other substance, and sometimes are specified by drug name, as in the case of marijuana. As the statute has been amended since its initial passage in 1970, the penalties have been altered by Congress. The charts on pages 8 and 9 are an overview of the penalties for trafficking or unlawful distribution of controlled substances. This is not inclusive of the penalties provided under the CSA.

User Accountability/Personal Use Penalties

On November 19, 1988, Congress passed the Anti-Drug Abuse Act of 1988, P. L. 100690. Two sections of this Act represent the Federal Government's attempt to reduce drug abuse by dealing not just with the person who sells the illegal drug, but also with the person who buys it. The first new section is titled "User Accountability" and is codified at 21 U.S.C. § 862 and various sections of Title 42, U.S.C. The second involves "personal use amounts" of illegal drugs, and is codified at 21 U.S.C. § 844a.

User Accountability

The purpose of User Accountability is to not only make the public aware of the Federal Government's position on drug abuse, but to describe new programs intended to decrease drug abuse by holding drug abusers personally responsible for their illegal activities, and imposing civil penalties on those who violate drug laws.

It is important to remember that these penalties are in addition to the criminal penalties drug abusers are already given, and do not replace those criminal penalties.

The new User Accountability programs call for more instruction in schools, kindergarten through senior high, to educate children on the dangers of drug abuse. These programs will include participation by students, parents, teachers, local businesses and the local, state and Federal Government.

User Accountability also targets businesses interested in doing business with the Federal Government. This program requires those businesses to maintain a drug free workplace, principally through educating employees on the dangers of drug abuse, and by informing employees of the penalties they face if they engage in illegal drug activity on company property.

There is also a provision in the law that makes public housing projects drug-free by evicting those residents who allow their units to be used for illegal drug activity, and denies Federal benefits, such as housing assistance and student loans, to individuals convicted of illegal drug activity. Depending on the offense, an individual may be prohibited from ever receiving any benefit provided by the Federal Government.

Personal Use Amounts

This section of the 1988 Act allows the government to punish minor drug offenders without giving the offender a criminal record if the offender is in possession of only a small amount of drugs. This law is designed to impact the "user" of illicit drugs, while simultaneously saving the government the costs of a full-blown criminal investigation.

Under this section, the government has the option of imposing only a civil fine on individuals possessing only a small quantity of an illegal drug. Possession of this small quantity, identified as a "personal use amount" carries a civil fine of up to $10,000.

In determining the amount of the fine in a particular case, the drug offender's income and assets will be considered. This is accomplished through an administrative proceeding rather than a criminal trial, thus reducing the exposure of the offender to the entire criminal justice system, and reducing the costs to the offender and the government.

The value of this section is that it allows the government to punish a minor drug offender without saddling the offender with a criminal record. This section also gives the drug offender the opportunity to fully redeem himself or herself, and have all public record of the proceeding destroyed. If this was the drug offender's first offense, and the offender has paid all fines, can pass a drug test, and has not been convicted of a crime after three years, the offender can request that all proceedings be dismissed.

If the proceeding is dismissed, the drug offender can lawfully say he or she had never been prosecuted, either criminally or civilly, for a drug offense.

Congress has imposed two limitations on this section's use. It may not be used if (1) the drug offender has been previously convicted of a Federal or state drug offense; or (2) the offender has already been fined twice under this section.

NARCOTICS

The term narcotic, derived from the Greek word for stupor, originally referred to a variety of substances that induced sleep. In a legal context, narcotic refers to opium, opium derivatives and their semisynthetic or totally synthetic substitutes. Cocaine and coca leaves, which are classified as "narcotics" in the Controlled Substances Act (CSA), are technically not narcotics and are discussed in the section on stimulants.

Narcotics can be administered in a variety of ways. Some are taken orally, transdermally (skin patches) or injected. They are also available in suppositories. As drugs of abuse, they are often smoked, sniffed or self-administered by the more direct routes of subcutaneous ("skin popping") and intravenous ("mainlining") injection.

Drug effects depend heavily on the dose, route of administration, previous exposure to the drug and the expectation of the user. Aside from their clinical use in the treatment of pain, cough suppression and acute diarrhea, narcotics produce a general sense of well-being by reducing tension, anxiety, and aggression. These effects are helpful in a therapeutic setting but contribute to their abuse.

Narcotic use is associated with a variety of unwanted effects including drowsiness, inability to concentrate, apathy, lessened physical activity, constriction of the pupils, dilation of the subcutaneous blood vessels causing flushing of the face and neck, constipation, nausea and vomiting and, most significantly, respiratory depression. As the dose is increased, the subjective, analgesic, and toxic effects become more pronounced. Except in cases of acute intoxication, there is no loss of motor coordination or slurred speech as occurs with many depressants.

Among the hazards of illicit drug use is the ever increasing risk of infection, disease and overdose. Medical complications common among narcotic abusers arise primarily from adulterants found in street drugs and in the non-sterile practices of injecting. Skin, lung and brain abscesses, endocarditis, hepatitis and AIDS are commonly found among narcotic abusers. Since there is no simple way to determine the purity of a drug that is sold on the street, the effects of illicit narcotic use are unpredictable and can be fatal.

With repeated use of narcotics, tolerance and dependence develop. The development of tolerance is characterized by a shortened duration and a decreased intensity of analgesia, euphoria and sedation which creates the need to administer progressively larger doses to attain the desired effect. Tolerance does not develop uniformly for all actions of these drugs, giving rise to a number of toxic effects. Although the lethal dose is increased significantly in tolerant users, there is always a dose at which death can occur from respiratory depression.

Physical dependence refers to an alteration of nor" mal body functions that necessitates the continued presence of a drug in order to prevent the withdrawal or abstinence syndrome. The intensity and character of the physical symptoms experienced during withdrawal are directly related to the particular drug of abuse, the total daily dose, the interval between doses, the duration of use and the health and personality of the addict. In general, narcotics with shorter durations of action tend to produce shorter, more intense withdrawal symptoms, while drugs that produce longer narcotic effects have prolonged symptoms that tend to be less severe.

The withdrawal symptoms experienced from heroin/morphine-like addiction are usually experienced shortly before the time of the next scheduled dose. Early symptoms include watery eyes, runny nose, yawning and sweating. Restlessness, irritability, loss of appetite, tremors and severe sneezing appear as the syndrome progresses. Severe depression and vomiting are not uncommon. The heart rate and blood pressure are elevated. Chills alternating with flushing and excessive sweating are also characteristic symptoms. Pains in the bones and muscles of the back and extremities occur as do muscle spasms and kicking movements, which may be the source of the expression "kicking the habit." At any point during this process, a suitable narcotic can be administered that will dramatically reverse the withdrawal symptoms. Without intervention, the syndrome will run its course and most of the overt physical symptoms will disappear within 7 to 10 days.

The psychological dependence that is associated with narcotic addiction is complex and protracted. Long after the physical need for the drug has passed, the addict may continue to think and talk about the use of drugs. There is a high probability that relapse will occur after narcotic withdrawal when neither the physical environment nor the behavioral motivators that contributed to the abuse have been altered.

There are two major patterns of narcotic abuse or dependence seen in the U.S. One involves individuals whose drug use was initiated within the context of medical treatment who escalate their dose through "doctor shopping" or branch out to illicit drugs. A very small percentage of addicts are in this group

The other more common pattern of abuse is initiated outside the therapeutic setting with experimental or recreational use of narcotics. The majority of individuals in this category may abuse narcotics sporadically for months or even years. These occasional users are called "chippers." Although they are neither tolerant of nor dependent on narcotics, the social, medical and legal consequences of their behavior is very serious. Some experimental users will escalate their narcotic use and will eventually become dependent, both physically and psychologically. The earlier drug use begins, the more likely it is to progress to abuse and dependence. Heroin use among males in inner cities is generally initiated in adolescence and dependence develops in about 1or 2 years.

Narcotics of Natural Origin

The poppy *Papaver somniferum* is the source for non-synthetic narcotics. It was grown in the Mediterranean region as early as 5000 B.C., and has since been cultivated in a number of countries throughout the world. The milky fluid that seeps from incisions in the unripe seedpod of this poppy has, since ancient times, been scraped by hand and air dried to produce what is known as opium. A more modern method of harvesting is by the industrial poppy straw process of extracting alkaloids from the mature dried plant. The extract may be in liquid, solid or powder form, although most poppy straw concentrate available commercially is a fine brownish powder. More than 500 tons of opium or their equivalents in poppy straw concentrate are legally imported into the U.S. annually for legitimate medical use.

Opium - There were no legal restrictions on the importation or use of opium until the early 1900s. In the United States, the unrestricted availability of opium, the influx of opium smoking immigrants from the Orient, and the invention of the hypodermic needle contributed to the more severe variety of compulsive drug abuse seen at the turn of this century. In those days, medicines often contained opium without any warning label. Today there are state, federal and international laws governing the production and distribution of narcotic substances.

Although opium is used in the form of paragoric to treat diarrhea, most opium imported into the United States is broken down into its alkaloid constituents. These alkaloids are divided into two distinct chemical classes, phenanthrenes and isoquinolines. The principal phenanthrenes are morphine, codeine and thebaine, while the isoquinolines have no significant central nervous system effects and are not regulated under the CSA.

Morphine - Morphine, the principal constituent of opium, can range in concentration from 4 to 21 percent (note: commercial opium is standardized to contain 10% morphine). It is one of the most effective drugs known for the relief of pain, and remains the standard against which new analgesics are measured. Morphine is marketed in a variety of forms including oral solutions (Roxanol), sustained release tablets (MSIR and MS-Contin), suppositories and injectable preparations. It may be administered orally, subcutaneously, intramuscularly, or intravenously, the latter method being the one most frequently used by addicts. Tolerance and physical dependence develop rapidly in the user. Only a small part of the morphine obtained from opium is used directly; most of it is converted to codeine and other derivatives.

Codeine - This alkaloid is found in opium in concentrations ranging from 0.7 to 2.5 percent. Most codeine used in the U.S. is produced from morphine. Compared to morphine, codeine produces less analgesia, sedation and respiratory depression and is frequently taken orally. Codeine is medically prescribed for the relief of moderate pain. It is made into tablets either alone or in combination with aspirin or acetaminophen (Tylenol). Codeine is an effective cough suppressant and is found in a number of liquid preparations. Codeine products are also used to a lesser extent, as an injectable solution for the treatment of pain. It is by far the most widely used naturally occurring narcotic in medical treatment in the world. Codeine products are encountered on the illicit market frequently in combination with glutethimide (Doriden) or carisoprodol (Soma).

Thebaine - A minor constituent of opium, thebaine is chemically similar to both morphine and codeine, but produces stimulatory rather than depressant effects. Thebaine is not used therapeutically, but is converted into a variety of compounds including codeine, hydrocodone, oxycodone, oxymorphone, nalbuphine, naloxone, naltrexone and buprenorphine. It is controlled in Schedule II of the CSA as well as under international law.

Semi-Synthetic Narcotics

The following narcotics are among the more significant substances that have been derived by modification of the phenanthrene alkaloids contained in opium:

Heroin - First synthesized from morphine in 1874, heroin was not extensively used in medicine until the beginning of this century. Commercial production of the new pain remedy was first started in 1898. While it received widespread acceptance from the medical profession, physicians remained unaware of its potential for addiction for years. The first comprehensive control of heroin in the United States was established with the Harrison Narcotic Act of 1914.

Pure heroin is a white powder with a bitter taste. Most illicit heroin is a powder which may vary in color from white to dark brown because of impurities left from the manufacturing process or the presence of additives. Pure heroin is rarely sold on the street. A "bag"-slang for a single dosage unit of heroin-may contain 100 mg of powder, only a portion of which is heroin; the remainder could be sugars, starch, powdered milk, or quinine. Traditionally the purity of heroin in a bag has ranged from 1 to 10 percent; more recently heroin purity has ranged from 1 to 98 percent, with a national average of 35 percent.

Another form of heroin known as "black tar" has also become increasingly available in the western United States. The color and consistency of black tar heroin result from the crude processing methods used to illicitly manufacture heroin in Mexico. Black tar heroin may be sticky like roofing tar or hard like coal, and its color may vary from dark brown to black. Black tar heroin is often sold on the street in its tar-like state at purities ranging from 20 to 80 percent. Black tar heroin is most frequently dissolved, diluted and injected.

The typical heroin user today consumes more heroin than a typical user did just a decade ago, which is not surprising given the higher purity currently available at the street level. Until recently, heroin in the United States almost exclusively was injected either intravenously, subcutaneously (skin-popping), or intramuscularly. Injection is the most practical and efficient way to administer low-purity heroin. The availability of higher purity heroin has meant that users now can snort or smoke the narcotic. Evidence suggests that heroin snorting is widespread or increasing in those areas of the country where high-purity heroin is available, generally in the northeastern United States. This method of administration may be more appealing to new users because it eliminates both the fear of acquiring syringe-borne diseases such as HIV / AIDS and hepatitis, and the historical stigma attached to intravenous heroin use.

Hydromorphone - Hydromorphone (Dilaudid) is marketed both in tablet and injectable forms. Its analgesic potency is from two to eight times that of morphine. Much sought after by narcotic addicts, hydromorphone is usually obtained by the abuser through fraudulent prescriptions or theft. The tablets are dissolved and injected as a substitute for heroin

Oxycodone - Oxycodone is synthesized from thebaine. It is similar to codeine, but is more potent and has a higher dependence potential. It is effective orally and is marketed in combination with aspirin (Percodan) or acetaminophen (Percocet) for the relief of pain. Addicts take these tablets orally or dissolve them in water, filter out the insoluble material, and "mainline" the active drug.

Hydrocodone - Hydrocodone is an orally active analgesic and antitussive Schedule II narcotic which is marketed in multi-ingredient Schedule III products. The therapeutic dose of 5-10 mg is pharmacologically equivalent to 60 mg of oral morphine. Sales and production of this drug have increased significantly in recent years as have diversion and illicit use. Trade names include Anexsia, Hycodan, Hycomine, Lorcet, Lortab, Tussionex, Tylox and Vicodin. These are available as tablets, capsules and/or syrups.

Synthetic Narcotics

In contrast to the pharmaceutical products derived directly or indirectly from narcotics of natural origin, synthetic narcotics are produced entirely within the laboratory. The continuing search for products that retain the analgesic properties of morphine without the consequent dangers of tolerance and dependence has yet to yield a product that is not susceptible to abuse. A number of clandestinely-produced drugs as well as drugs that have accepted medical uses fall into this category.

Meperidine - Introduced as a potent analgesic in the 1930s, meperidine produces effects that are similar but not identical to morphine (shorter duration of action and reduced antitussive and antidiarrheal actions). Currently it is used for the relief of moderate to severe pain, particularly in obstetrics and post-operative situations. Meperdine is available in tablets, syrups and injectable forms (Demerol). Several analogues of meperidine have been clandestinely produced. One noteworthy analogue is a preparation with a neurotoxic by-product that has produced irreversible Parkinsonism.

Methadone and Related Drugs - German scientist's synthesized methadone during World War II because of a shortage of morphine. Although chemically unlike morphine or heroin, methadone produces many of the same effects. Introduced into the United States in 1947 as an analgesic (Dolophine), it is primarily used today for the treatment of narcotic addiction (Methadone). The effects of methadone are longer-lasting than those of morphine based drugs. Methadone's effects can last up to 24 hours, thereby permitting administration only once a day in heroin detoxification and maintenance programs. Methadone is almost as effective when administered orally as it is by injection. Tolerance and dependence may develop, and withdrawal symptoms, though they develop more slowly and are less severe than those of morphine and more slowly and are less severe than those of morphine and heroin, are more prolonged. Ironically, methadone used to control narcotic addiction is frequently encountered on the illicit market and has been associated with a number of overdose deaths.

Closely related to methadone, the synthetic compound levo-alphacetylmethadol or LAAM (ORLAAM) has an even longer duration of action (from 48 to 72 hours), permitting a reduction in frequency of use. In 1994 it was approved as a treatment of narcotic addiction. Buprenorphine (Buprenex), a semi-synthetic Schedule V narcotic analgesic derived from thebaine, is currently being investigated as a treatment of narcotic addiction.

Another close relative of methadone is dextropropoxyphene, first marketed in 1957 under the trade name of Darvon. Oral analgesic potency is one-half to one-third that of codeine, with 65 mg approximately equivalent to about 600 mg of aspirin. Dextroproxyphene is prescribed for relief of mild to moderate pain. Bulk dextropropoxyphene is in Schedule II, while preparations containing it are in Schedule IV. More than 100 tons of dextropropoxyphene are produced in the U.S. annually, and more than 25 million prescriptions are written for the products. This narcotic is associated with a number of toxic side effects and is among the top 10 drugs reported by medical examiners in drug abuse deaths.

Fentanyl - First synthesized in Belgium in the late 1950s, fentanyl was introduced into clinical practice in the 1960s as an intravenous anesthetic under the trade name of Sublimaze. Thereafter, two other fentanyl analogues were introduced: alfentanil (Alfenta), an ultra-short (5-10 minutes) acting analgesic, and sufentanil (Sufenta), an exceptionally potent analgesic for use in heart surgery. Today fentanyls are extensively used for anesthesia and analgesia. Illicit use of pharmaceutical fentanyls first appeared in the mid-1970s in the medical community and continues to be a problem in the U.S. To date, over 12 different analogues of fentanyl have been produced clandestinely and identified in the U.S. drug traffic. The biological effects of the fentanyls are indistinguishable from those of heroin with the exception that the fentanyls may be hundreds of times more potent. Fentanyls are most commonly used by intravenous administration, but like heroin, they may be smoked or snorted.

Pentazocine - The effort to find an effective analgesic that is less dependence-producing led to the development of pentazocine (Tal win). Introduced as an analgesic in 1967, it was frequently encountered in the illicit trade, usually in combination with tripelennamine and placed into Schedule IV in 1979. An attempt at reducing the abuse of this drug was made with the introduction of Talwin Nx. This product contains a quantity of antagonist sufficient to counteract the morphine-like effects of pentazocine if the tablets are dissolved and injected.

DEPRESSANTS

Historically, people of almost every culture have used chemical agents to induce sleep, relieve stress, and allay anxiety. While alcohol is one of the oldest and most universal agents used for these purposes, hundreds of substances have been developed that produce central nervous system (CNS) depression. These drugs have been referred to as "downers," sedatives, hypnotics, minor tranquilizers, anxiolytics, and antianxiety medications. Unlike most other classes of drugs of abuse, depressants, except for methaqualone, are rarely produced in clandestine laboratories. Generally, legitimate pharmaceutical products are diverted to the illicit market.

Although a number of depressants (i.e., chloral hydrate, glutethimide, meprobamate and methaqualone) have been important players in the milieu of depressant use and abuse, two major groups of depressants have dominated the licit and illicit market for nearly a century, first barbiturates and now benzodiazepines.

Barbiturates were very popular in the first half of this century. In moderate amounts, these drugs produce a state of intoxication that is remarkably similar to alcohol intoxication. Symptoms include slurred speech, loss of motor coordination and impaired judgment. Depending on the dose, frequency, and duration of use, one can rapidly develop tolerance, physical dependence and psychological dependence on barbiturates. With the development of tolerance, the margin of safety between the effective dose and the lethal dose becomes very narrow. That is, in order to obtain the same level of intoxication, the tolerant abuser may raise his or her dose to a level that can produce coma and death. Although many individuals have taken barbiturates therapeutically without harm, concern about the addiction potential of barbiturates and the ever-increasing numbers of fatalities associated with them led to the development of alternative medications. Today, only about 20% of all depressant prescriptions in the U.S. are for barbiturates.

Benzodiazepines were first marketed in the 1960s. Touted as much safer depressants with far less addiction potential than barbiturates, these drugs today account for about 30% of all prescriptions for controlled substances. It has only been recently that an awareness has developed that benzodiazepines share many of the undesirable side effects of the barbiturates. A number of toxic CNS effects are seen with chronic high dose benzodiazepine therapy. These include headache, irritability, confusion, memory impairment, depression, insomnia and tremor. The risk of developing over-sedation, dizziness and confusion increases substantially with higher doses of benzodiazepines. Prolonged use can lead to physical dependence even at recommended dosages. Unlike barbiturates, large doses of benzodiazepines are rarely fatal unless combined with other drugs or alcohol. Although primary abuse of benzodiazepines is well documented, abuse of these drugs usually occurs as part of a pattern of multiple drug abuse. For example, heroin or cocaine abusers will use benzodiazepines and other depressants to augment their "high" or alter the side effects associated with over-stimulation or narcotic withdrawal.

There are marked similarities among the withdrawal symptoms seen with all drugs classified as depressants. In its mildest form, the withdrawal syndrome may produce insomnia and anxiety, usually the same symptoms that initiated the drug use. With a greater level of dependence, tremors and weakness are also present, and in its most severe form, the withdrawal syndrome can cause seizures and delirium. Unlike the withdrawal syndrome seen with most other drugs of abuse, withdrawal from depressants can be life-threatening

Chloral Hydrate

The oldest of the hypnotic (sleep inducing) depressants, chloral hydrate was first synthesized in 1832. Marketed as syrups or soft gelatin capsules, chloral hydrate takes effect in a relatively short time (30 minutes) and will induce sleep in about an hour. A solution of chloral hydrate and alcohol
constituted the infamous "knockout drops" or "Mickey Finn." At therapeutic doses, chloral· hydrate has little effect on respiration and blood pressure but, a toxic dose produces severe respiratory depression and very low blood pressure. Although chloral hydrate is still encountered today, its use declined with the introduction of the barbiturates

Barbiturates

Barbiturates (derivatives of barbituric acid) were first introduced for medical use in the early 1900s. More than 2,500 barbiturates have been synthesized, and in the height of their popularity about 50 were marketed for human use. Today, only about a dozen are used. Barbiturates produce a wide spectrum of CNS depression, from mild sedation to coma, and have been used as sedatives, hypnotics, anesthetics and anticonvulsants.

The primary differences among many of these products are how fast they produce an effect and how long those effects last. Barbiturates are classified as ultrashort, short, intermediate and long-acting.

The ultrashort-acting barbiturates produce anesthesia within about one minute after intravenous administration. Those in current medical use are methohexital (Brevital), thiamylal (Surital) and thiopental (Pentothal).

Barbiturate abusers prefer the short-acting and intermediate-acting barbiturates pentobarbital (Nembutal), secobarbital (Seconal) and amobarbital (Amytal). Other short- and intermediate-acting barbiturates are butalbital (Fiorinal, Fioricet), butabarbital (Butisol), talbutal (Lotusate) and aprobarbital (Alurate). After oral administration, the onset of action is from 15 to 40 minutes and the effects last up to 6 hours. These drugs are primarily used for sedation or to induce sleep. Veterinarians use pentobarbital for anesthesia and euthanasia.

Long-acting barbiturates include phenobarbital (Luminal) and mephobarbital (Mebaral). Effects of these drugs are realized in about one hour and last for about 12 hours and are used primarily for daytime sedation and the treatment of seizure disorders or mild anxiety.

Glutethimide and Methqualone

Glutethimide (Doriden) was introduced in 1954 and methaqualone (Quaalude, Sopor) in 1965 as safe barbiturate substitutes. Experience showed, however, that their addiction liability and the severity of withdrawal symptoms were similar to those of barbiturates. By 1972, "luding out," taking methaqualone with wine, was a popular college pastime. Excessive use leads to tolerance, dependence and withdrawal symptoms similar to those of barbiturates. Overdose by glutethimide and methaqualone is more difficult to treat than barbiturate overdose, and deaths have frequently occurred. In the United States, the marketing of methaqualone pharmaceutical products stopped in 1984 and methaqualone was transferred to Schedule I of the CSA. In 1991, glutethimide was transferred into Schedule II in response to an upsurge in the prevalence of diversion, abuse and overdose deaths.

Meprobamate

Meprobamate was introduced as an antianxiety agent in 1955 and is prescribed primarily to treat anxiety, tension and associated muscle spasms. More than 50 tons are distributed annually in the U.S. under its generic name and brand names such as Miltown and Equanil. Its onset and duration of action are similar to the intermediate acting barbiturates; however, therapeutic doses of meprobamate produce less sedation and toxicity than barbiturates. Excessive use can result in psychological and physical dependence.

Benzodiazepines

The benzodiazepine family of depressants is used therapeutically to produce sedation, induce sleep, relieve anxiety and muscle spasms and to prevent seizures. In general, benzodiazepines act as hypnotics in high doses, as anxiolytics in moderate doses and as sedatives in low doses. Of the drugs marketed in the United States that affect CNS function, benzodiazepines are among the widely prescribed medications and, unfortunately, are frequently abused. Fifteen members of this group are presently marketed in the United States and an additional twenty are marketed in other countries.

Like the barbiturates, benzodiazepines differ from one another in how fast they take effect and how long the effects last. Shorter acting benzodiazepines, used to manage insomnia, include estazolam (ProSom), flurazepam (Dalmane), quazepam (Doral), temazepam (Restoril) and triazolam (Halcion).

Benzodiazepines with longer durations of action include alprazolam (Xanax), chlordiazepoxide (Librium), clorazepate (Tranxene), diazepam (Valium), halazepam (Paxipam), lorazepam (Ativan), oxazepam (Serax) and prazepam (Centrax). These longer acting drugs are primarily used for the treatment of general anxiety. Midazolam (Versed) is available in the U.S. only in an injectable form for an adjunct to anesthesia. Clonazepam (Klonopin) is recommended for use in the treatment of seizure disorders.

Flunitrazepam (Rohypnol), which produces diazepam-like effects, is becoming increasingly popular among young people as a drug of abuse. The drug is not marketed legally in the United States, but is smuggled in by traffickers.

Benzodiazepines are classified in the CSA as Schedule IV depressants. Repeated use of large doses or, in some cases, daily use of therapeutic doses of benzodiazepines is associated with physical dependence. The withdrawal syndrome is similar to that of alcohol withdrawal and is generally more unpleasant and longer lasting than narcotic withdrawal and frequently requires hospitalization. Abrupt cessation of benzodiazepines is not recommended and tapering-down the dose eliminates many of the unpleasant symptoms.

Given the number of people who are prescribed benzodiazepines, relatively few patients increase their dosage or engage in drugseeking behavior. However, those individuals who do abuse benzodiazepines often maintain their drug supply by getting prescriptions from several doctors, forging prescriptions or buying diverted pharmaceutical products on the illicit market. Abuse is frequently associated with adolescents and young adults who take benzodiazepines to obtain a "high." This intoxicated state results in reduced inhibition and impaired judgment. Concurrent use of a1cohol or other depressants with benzodiazepines can be life-threatening. Abuse of benzodiazepines is particularly high among heroin and cocaine abusers. Approximately 50 percent of people entering treatment for narcotic or cocaine addiction also report abusing benzodiazepines.

STIMULANTS

Stimulants are sometimes referred to as "uppers" and reverse the effects of fatigue on both mental and physical tasks. Two commonly used stimulants are nicotine, found in tobacco products, and caffeine, an active ingredient in coffee, tea, some soft drinks and many non-prescription medicines. Used in moderation, these substances tend to relieve malaise and increase alertness. Although the use of these products has been an accepted part of our culture, the recognition of their adverse effects has resulted in a proliferation of caffeine-free products and efforts to discourage cigarette smoking.

A number of stimulants, however, are under the regulatory control of the CSA. Some of these controlled substances are available by prescription for legitimate medical use in the treatment of obesity, narcolepsy and attention deficit hyperactivity disorders. As drugs of abuse, stimulants are frequently taken to produce a sense of exhilaration, enhance self-esteem, improve mental and physical performance, increase activity, reduce appetite, produce prolonged wakefulness, and to "get high." They are recognized as among the most potent agents of reward and reinforcement that underlie the problem of dependence.

Stimulants are both diverted from legitimate channels and clandestinely manufactured exclusively for the illicit market. They are taken orally, sniffed, smoked and injected. Smoking, snorting or injecting stimulants produces a sudden sensation known. as a "rush" or a "flash." Abuse is often associated with a pattern of binge use that is, consuming large doses of stimulants sporadically. Heavy users may inject themselves every few hours, continuing until they have depleted their drug supply or reached a point of delirium, psychosis and physical exhaustion. During this period of heavy use, all other interests become secondary to recreating the initial euphoric rush. Tolerance can develop rapidly, and both physical and psychological dependence occur. Abrupt cessation, even after a weekend binge, is commonly followed by depression, anxiety, drug craving and extreme fatigue ("crash").

Therapeutic levels of stimulants can produce exhilaration, extended wakefulness and loss of appetite. These effects are greatly intensified when large doses of stimulants are taken. Physical side effects-including dizziness, tremor, headache, flushed skin, chest pain with palpitations, excessive sweating, vomiting and abdominal cramps-may occur as a result of taking too large a dose at one time or taking large doses over an extended period of time. Psychological effects include agitation, hostility, panic, aggression and suicidal or homicidal tendencies. Paranoia, sometimes accompanied by both auditory and visual hallucinations, may also occur. In overdose, unless there is medical intervention, high fever, convulsions and car- diovascular collapse may precede death. Because accidental death is partially due to the effects of stimulants on the body's cardiovascular and temperature-regulating systems, physical exertion increases the hazards of stimulant use.

Cocaine

Cocaine, the most potent stimulant of natural origin, is extracted from the leaves of the coca plant (Erythroxylon coca) which is indigenous to the Andean highlands of South America. Natives in this region chew or brew coca leaves into a tea for refreshment and to relieve fatigue similar to the customs of chewing tobacco and drinking tea or coffee.

Pure cocaine was first isolated in the 1880s and used as a local anesthetic in eye surgery. It was particularly useful in surgery of the nose and throat because of its ability to provide   anesth-

anesthesia as well as to constrict blood vessels and limit bleeding. Many of its therapeutic applications are now obsolete due to the development of safer drugs.

Illicit cocaine is usually distributed as a white crystalline powder or as an off-white chunky material. The powder, usually cocaine hydrochloride, is often diluted with a variety of substances, the most common of which are sugars such as lactose, inositol and mannitol, and local anesthetics such as lidocaine. The adulteration increases the volume and thus multiplies profits. Cocaine hydrochloride is generally snorted or dissolved in water and injected. It is rarely smoked.

"Crack," the chunk or "rock" form of cocaine, is a ready-to-use freebase. On the illicit market it is sold in small, inexpensive dosage units that are smoked. With crack came a dramatic increase in drug abuse problems and violence. Smoking delivers large quantities of cocaine to the lungs producing effects comparable to intravenous injection; these effects are felt almost immediately after smoking, are very intense, and are quickly over. Once introduced in the mid-1980s, crack abuse spread rapidly and made the cocaine experience available to anyone with $10 and access to a dealer. In addition to other toxicities associated with cocaine abuse, cocaine smokers suffer from acute respiratory problems including cough, shortness of breath, and severe chest painswitll lung trauma and bleeding.

The intensity of the psychological effects of cocaine, as with most psychoactive drugs, depends on the dose and rate of entry to the brain. Cocaine reaches the brain through the snorting method in three to five minutes. Intravenous injection of cocaine produces a rush in 15 to 30 seconds and smoking produces an almost immediate intense experience. The euphoric effects of cocaine are almost indistinguishable from those of amphetamine, although they do not last as long. These intense effects can be followed by a dysphoric crash. To avoid the fatigue and the depression of "coming down," frequent repeated doses are taken. Excessive doses of cocaine may lead to seizures and death from respiratory failure, stroke, cerebral hemorrhage or heart failure. There is no specific antidote for cocaine overdose.

According to the 1993 Household Drug Survey, the number of Americans who used cocaine within the preceding month of the survey numbered about 1.3 million; occasional users (those who used cocaine less often than monthly) numbered at approximately 3 million, down from 8.1 million in 1985. The number of weekly users has remained steady at around a half million since 1983.

Amphetamines

Amphetamine, dextroamphetamine and methamphetamine are collectively referred to as amphetamines. Their chemical properties and actions are so similar that even experienced users have difficulty knowing which drug they have taken.

Amphetamine was first marketed in the 1930s as Benzedrine in an over-the-counter inhaler to treat nasal congestion. By 1937 amphetamine was available by prescription in tablet form and was used in the treatment of the sleeping disorder narcolepsy and the behavioral syndrome called minimal brain dysfunction (MBD), which today is called attention deficit hyperactivity disorder (ADHD). During World War II, amphetamine was widely used to keep the fighting men going; both dextroamphetamine (Dexedrine) and methamphetamine (Methedrine) became readily available. As use of amphetamines spread, so did their abuse. Amphetamines became a cureall for helping truckers to complete their long routes without falling asleep, for weight control, for helping athletes to perform better and train longer, and for treating mild depression. Intravenous amphetamine abuse spread among a subculture known as "speed freaks." With experience, it became evident that the dangers of abuse of these drugs outweighed most of their therapeutic uses.

Increased control measures were initiated in 1965 with amendments to the federal food and drug laws to curb the black market in amphetamines. Many pharmaceutical amphetamine products were removed from the market and doctors prescribed those that remained less freely. In order to
meet the everincreasing black market demand for amphetamines, clandestine laboratory's. production mushroomed, especially methamphetamine laboratories on the West Coast. Today, most amphetamines distributed to the black market are produced in clandestine laboratories.

Amphetamines are generally taken orally or injected. However, the addition of "ice," the slang name for crystallized methamphetamine hydrochloride, has promoted smoking as another mode of administration. Just as "crack" is smokable cocaine, "ice" is smokable methamphetamine. Both drugs are highly addictive and toxic.

The effects of amphetamines, especially methamphetamine, are similar to cocaine, but their onset is slower and their duration is longer. In general, chronic abuse produces a psychosis that resembles schizophrenia and is characterized by paranoia, picking at the skin, preoccupation with one's own thoughts, and auditory and visual hallucinations. Violent and erratic behavior is frequently seen among chronic abusers of amphetamines.

Methcathinone

Methcathinone is one of the more recent drugs of abuse in the U.S. and was placed into Schedule I of the CSA in 1993. Known on the streets as "Cat," it is a structural analogue of methamphetamine and cathinone. Clandestinely manufactured, methcathinone is almost exclusively sold in the stable and highly water soluble hydrochloride salt form. It is most commonly snorted, although it can be taken orally by mixing it with a beverage or diluted in water and injected intravenously. Methcathinone has an abuse potential equivalent to methamphetamine, and produces amphetamine-like activity including superabundant energy, hyperactivity, extended wakefulness and loss of appetite. Pleasant effects include a burst of energy, speeding of the mind, increased feelings of invincibility and euphoria. Unpleasant effects include anxiety, tremor, insomnia, weight loss, dehydration, sweating, stomach pains, pounding heart, nose bleeds and body aches. Toxic levels may produce convulsions, paranoia, and hallucinations. Like other CNS stimulants, binges are usually followed by a "crash" with periods of variable depression.

Khat

For centuries, khat, the fresh young leaves of the Catha edulis shrub, has been consumed where the plant is cultivated, primarily in East Africa and the Arabian Peninsula. There, chewing khat predates the use of coffee and is used in a similar social context. Chewed in moderation, khat alleviates fatigue and reduces appetite. Compulsive use may result in manic behavior with grandiose delusions or in a paranoid type of illness, some- times accompanied by hallucinations.

Khat has been brought into the U.S. and other countries for use by emigrants from the source countries. It contains a number of chemicals among which are two controlled substances, cathinone (Schedule I) and cathine (Schedule IV). As the leaves mature or dry, cathinone is converted to cathine which significantly reduces its stimulatory properties.

Methylphenidate (Ritalin)

The primary, legitimate medical use of methylphenidate (Ritalin) is to treat attention deficit disorders in children. As with other Schedule II stimulants, the abuse of methylphenidate may produce the same effects as the abuse of cocaine or the amphetamines. It has been reported that the psychosis of chronic methylphenidate intoxication is identical to the paranoid psychosis of amphetamine intoxication. Unlike other stimulants, however, methylphenidate has not been clandestinely produced, although abuse of this substance has been well documented among narcotic addicts who dissolve the tablets in water and inject the mixture. Complications arising from this practice are common due to the insoluble fillers used in the tablets. When injected, these materials block small blood vessels, causing serious damage to the lung and retina of the eye.

Anorectic Drugs

A number of drugs have been developed and marketed to replace amphetamines as appetite suppressants. These anorectic drugs include benzphetamine (Didrex), diethylproprion (Tenuate, Tepanil), fenfluramine (Pondimin), mazindol (Sanorex, Mazanor), phendimetrazine (Bontril, Prelu-l, Plegine) and phentermine (Ionamin, AdipexP). They produce many of the effects of the amphetamines, but are generally less potent. All are controlled under the CSA because of the similarity of their effects to those of the amphetamines.

HALLUCINOGENS

Hallucinogens are amoung the oldest known group of drugs that have been used for their ability to alter human perception and mood. For centuries, many of the naturally occurring hallucinogens found in plants and fungi have been used for medical, social, and religious practices. In more recent years, a number of synthetic hallucinogens have been produced, some of which are much more potent than their naturally occurring counterparts.

The biochemical, pharmacological and physiological basis for hallucinogenic activity is not well understood. Even the name for this class of drugs is not ideal, since hallucinogens do not always produce hallucinations. However, taken in nontoxic dosages, these substances produce changes in perception, thought and mood. Physiological effects include elevated heart rate, increased blood pressure and dilated pupils. Sensory effects include perceptual distortions that vary with dose, setting and mood. Psychic effects include disorders of thought associated with time and space. Time may appear to stand still and forms and colors seem to change and take on new significance. This experience may be pleasurable or extremely frightening. It needs to be stressed that the effects of hallucinogens are unpredictable each time they are used.

Weeks or even months after some hallucinogens have been taken; the user may experience flashbacks-fragmentary recurrences of certain aspects of the drug experience in the absence of actually taking the drug. The occurrence of a flashback is unpredictable, but is more likely to occur during times of stress and seem to occur more frequently in younger individuals. With time, these episodes diminish and become less intense.

The abuse of hallucinogens in the United States reached a peak in the late 1960s. A subsequent decline in their use may be attributed to real or perceived hazards associated with taking these drugs. However, a resurgence of use of hallucinogens in the 1990s, especially at the junior high school level, is cause for concern.

There is a considerable body of literature that links the use of some of the hallucinogenic substances to neuronal damage in animals; however, there is no conclusive scientific data that links brain or chromosomal damage to the use of hallucinogens in humans. The most common danger of hallucinogen use is impaired judgment that often leads to rash decisions and accidents.

NATURALLY OCCURRING HALLUCINOGENS

Peyote and Mescaline

Peyote is a small, spineless cactus, Lophophora williamsii, whose principal active ingredient is the hallucinogen mescaline. From earliest recorded time, peyote has been used by natives in northern Mexico and southwestern United States as a part of traditional religious rites. The top of the cactus above ground-also referred to as the crown-consists of disc-shaped buttons that are cut from the roots and dried. These buttons are generally chewed or soaked in water to produce an intoxicating liquid. The hallucinogenic dose for mescaline is about 0.3 to 0.5 grams (equivalent to about 5 grams of dried peyote) and lasts about 12 hours. While peyote produced rich visual hallucinations which were important to the native peyote cults, the full spectrum of effects served as a chemically induced model of mental illness. Mescaline can be extracted from peyote or produced synthetically.

Psilocybin and Psilocyn

Psilocybin and psilocyn are both chemicals obtained from certain mushrooms found in Mexico and Central America. Like peyote, the mushrooms have been used in native rites for centuries. Dried mushrooms contain about 0.2 to 0.4 percent psilocybin and only trace amounts of psilocyn. The hallucinogenic dose of both substances is about 4 to 8 milligrams or about 2 grams of mushrooms with effects lasting for about six hours. Both psilocybin and psilocyn can be produced synthetically.

Dimethyltryptamine (DMT)

Dimethyltryptamine, (DMT) has a long history of use worldwide as it is found in a variety of plants and seeds and can also be produced synthetically. It is ineffective when taken orally unless combined with another drug that inhibits its metabolism. Generally it is sniffed, smoked or injected. The effective hallucinogenic dose in humans is about 50 to 100 milligrams and lasts for about 45 to 60 minutes. Because the effects last only about an hour, the experience was called a "businessman's trip."

A number of other hallucinogens have very similar structures and properties to those of DMT. Diethyltryptamine (DET), for example, is an analogue of DMT and produces the same pharmacological effects but is somewhat less potent than DMT. Alphaethyltryptamine (AET) is another tryptamine hallucinogen recently added to the list of Schedule I substances in the CSA.

LSD

Lysergic acid diethylamide (LSD) is the most potent and highly studied hallucinogen known to man. It was originally synthesized in 1938 by Dr. Albert Hoffman, but its hallucinogenic effects were unknown until 1943 when Hoffman accidently consumed some LSD. It was later found that an oral dose of as little as 0.025 mg (or 25 micrograms, equal to a few grains of salt) was capable of producing rich and vivid hallucinations.

Because of its structural similarity to a chemical present in the brain and its similarity in effects to certain aspects of psychosis, LSD was used as a research tool to study mental illness. Although there was a decline in its illicit use from its initial popularity in the 1960s, LSD is making a comeback in the 1990s. The average effective oral dose is from 20 to 80 micrograms with the effects of higher doses lasting for 10 to 12 hours. LSD is usually sold in the form of impregnated paper (blotter acid), tablets (microdots), or thin squares of gelatin (window panes).

Physical reactions may include dilated pupils, lowered body temperature, nausea, "goose bumps," profuse perspiration, increased blood sugar and rapid heart rate. During the first hour after ingestion, the user may experience visual changes with extreme changes in mood. In the hallucinatory state, the user may suffer impaired depth and time perception accompanied by distorted perception of the size and shape of objects, movements, color, sound, touch and the user's own body image. During this period, the user's ability to perceive objects through the senses is distorted. He may describe "hearing colors" and "seeing sounds." The ability to make sensible judgments and see common dangers is impaired, making the user susceptible to personal injury. He may also injure others by attempting to drive a car or by operating machinery. After an LSD "trip," the user may suffer acute anxiety or depression for a variable period of time. Flashbacks have been reported days or even months after taking the last dose.

DOM, DOB, MDA, MDMA and 2C-B

Many chemical variations of mescaline and amphetamine have been synthesized for their "feel good" effects. 4-Methyl-2, 5dimethoxyamphetamine (DaM) was introduced into the San Francisco drug scene in the late 1960s, and was nicknamed STP, an acronym for "Serenity, Tranquillity, and Peace." Doses of 1 to 3 milligrams generally produce mood alterations and minor perceptual alterations while larger doses can produce pronounced hallucinations that last from 8 to 10 hours.

Other illicitly manufactured analogues include 4-bromo- 2,5-dimethoxyamphetamine (DaB), 3,4-methylenedioxyamphetamine (MD A), 3,4- methy lenedioxymethamphetamine (MDMA, also referred to as Ecstasy or XTC) and 4-bromo-2,5-dimethoxyphenethylamine (2C-B, NEXUS). These drugs differ from one another in their potency, speed of onset, duration of action and their capacity to modify mood with or without producing overt hallucinations. These drugs are widely used at "raves." (Raves are large all-night dance parties held in unusual settings, such as warehouses or railroad yards, that feature computer-generated, high volume, pulsating music.) The drugs are usually taken orally, sometimes snorted and rarely injected. Because they are produced in clandestine laboratories, they are seldom pure and the amount in a capsule or tablet is likely to vary considerably.

Phencyclidine (PCP) and Related Drugs

In the 1950s, phencyclidine was investigated as an anesthetic but, due to the side effects of confusion and delirium, its development for human use was discontinued. It became commercially available for use as a veterinary anesthetic in the 1960s under the trade name of Semylan and was placed in Schedule III of the CSA. In 1978, due to considerable abuse of phencyclidine, it was transferred to Schedule II of the CSA and manufacturing of Semylan was discontinued. Today, virtually all of the phencyclidine encountered on the illicit market in the U.S. is produced in clandestine laboratories. Phencyclidine, more commonly known as PCP, is illicitly marketed under a number of other names including Angel Dust, Supergrass, Killer Weed, Embalming Fluid, and Rocket Fuel, reflecting the range of its bizarre and volatile effects. In its pure form, it is a white crystalline powder that readily dissolves in water. However, most PCP on the illicit market contains a number of contaminates as a result of makeshift manufacturing causing the color to range from tan to brown and the consistency from powder to a gummy mass. Although sold in tablets and capsules as well as in powder and liquid form, it is commonly applied to a leafy material, such as parsley, mint, oregano or marijuana, and smoked.

The drug's effects are as varied as its appearance. A moderate amount of PCP often causes the user to feel detached, distant and estranged from his surroundings. Numbness, slurred speech and loss of coordination may be accompanied by a sense of strength and invulnerability. A blank stare, rapid and involuntary eye movements, and an exaggerated gait are among the more observable effects. Auditory hallucinations, image distortion, severe mood disorders, and amnesia may also occur. In some users, PCP may cause acute anxiety and a feeling of impending doom, in others paranoia and violent hostility, and in some it may produce a psychoses indistinguishable from schizophrenia. PCP use is associated with a number of risks and many believe it to be one of the most dangerous drugs of abuse.

Modification of the manufacturing process may yield chemically related analogue capable of producing psychic effects similar to PCP. Four of these substances (N-ethyl-l-phenylcyclohexylamine or PCE, l-(phenylcyclohexyl)-pyrrolidine or PCP 1-[1-(2-thienyl)-cyclohexyl]-piperdine or TCP, and 1[l-(2-thienyl) cyclohexyl] pyrrolidine or TCP have been encountered on the illicit market and have been placed in Schedule I of the CSA. LSD is also a Schedule I hallucinogen.

CANNABIS

Cannabis sativa L., the hemp plant, grows wild throughout most of the tropic and temperate regions of the world. Prior to the advent of synthetic fibers, the cannabis plant was cultivated for the tough fiber of its stem. In the United States, cannabis is legitimately grown only for scientific research. In fact, since 1980, the United States has been the only country where cannabis is licitly cultivated for scientific research.

Cannabis contains chemicals called cannabinoids that are unique to the cannabis plant. Among the cannabinoids synthesized by the plant are cannabinol, cannabidiol, cannabinolidic acids, cannabigerol, cannabichromene, and several isomers of tetrahydrocannabinol. One of these, delta-9-tetrahydrocannabinol (THC), is believed to be responsible for most of the characteristic psychoactive effects of cannabis. Research has resulted in development and marketing of dronabinol (Marinol), a product containing synthetic THC, for the control of nausea and vomiting caused by chemotherapeutic agents used in the treatment of cancer, and to stimulate appetite in AIDS patients.

Cannabis products are usually smoked. Their effects are felt within minutes, reach their peak in 10 to 30 minutes, and may linger for two or three hours. The effects experienced often depend upon the experience and expectations of the individual user as well as the activity of the drug itself. Low doses tend to induce a sense of well-being and a dreamy state of relax at on, which may be accompanied by a more vivid sense of sight, smell, taste, and hearing as well as by subtle alterations in thought formation and expression. This state of intoxication may not be noticeable to an observer. However, driving, occupational or household accidents may result from a distortion of time and space relationships and impaired coordination. Stronger doses intensify reactions. The individual may experience shifting sensory imagery, rapidly fluctuating emotions, a flight of fragmentary thoughts with disturbed associations, an altered sense of selfidentity, impaired memory, and a dulling of attention despite an illusion of heightened insight. High doses may result in image distortion, a loss of personal identity, and fantasies and hallucinations.

Three drugs that come from cannabismarijuana, hashish, and hashish oil-are currently distributed on the U.S. illicit market. Having no currently accepted medical use in treatment in the United States, they remain under Schedule I of the CSA. Today, cannabis is carefully illicitly cultivated, both indoors and out, to maximize its THC content, thereby producing the greatest possible psychoactive effect.

Marijuana

Marijuana is the most commonly used illicit drug in America today. The term marijuana, as commonly used, refers to the leaves and flowering tops of the cannabis plant.

A tobacco-like substance produced by drying the leaves and flowering tops of the cannabis plant, marijuana varies significantly in its potency, depending on the source and selection of plant materials used. The form of marijuana known as sinsemilla (Spanish, sin semilla: without seed), derived from the unpollinated female cannabis plant, is preferred for its high THC content.

Marijuana is usually smoked in the form of loosely rolled cigarettes called joints or hollowed out commercial cigars called blunts. Joints and blunts may be laced with a number of adulterants including phencyclidine (PCP), substantially altering the effects and toxicity of these products. Street names for marijuana include pot, grass, weed, Mary Jane, Acupulco Gold, and reefer.

Although marijuana grown in the U.S. was once considered inferior because of a low concentration of THC, advancements in plant selection and cultivation have resulted in highly potent domestic marijuana. In 1974, the average THC content of illicit marijuana was less than one percent; in early 1994, potency averaged 5 percent. The THC of today's sinsemilla ranges up to 17 percent.

Marijuana contains known toxins and cancer-causing chemicals which are stored in fat cells for as long as several months. Marijuana users experience the same health problems as tobacco smokers, such as bronchitis, emphysema and bronchial asthma. Some of the effects of marijuana use also include increased heart rate, dryness of the mouth, reddening of the eyes, impaired motor skills and concentration, and frequently hunger and an increased desire for sweets. Extended use increases risk to the lungs and reproductive system, as well as suppression of the immune system. Occasionally hallucinations, fantasies and paranoia are reported.

Hashish

Hashish consists of the THC-rich resinous material of the cannabis plant, which is collected, dried, and then compressed into a variety of forms, such as balls, cakes, or cookie-like sheets. Pieces are then broken off, placed in pipes and smoked. The Middle East, North Africa, and Pakistan/Afghanistan are the main sources of hashish. The THC content of hashish that reached the United States, where demand is limited, averaged 6 percent in the -1990s.

Hash Oil

The term hash oil is used by illicit drug users and dealers but is a misnomer in suggesting any resemblance to hashish. Hash oil is produced by extracting the cannabinoids from plant material with a solvent. The color and odor of the resulting extract will vary, depending on the type of solvent used. Current samples of hash oil, a viscous liquid ranging from amber to dark brown in color, average about 15 percent The. In terms of its psychoactive effect, a drop or two of this liquid on a cigarette is equal to a single "joint" of marijuana.

STEROIDS

Anabolic steroid abuse has become a national concern. These drugs are used illicitly by weight lifters, body builders, long distance runners, cyclists and others who claim that these drugs give them a competitive advantage and/or improve their physical appearance. Once viewed as a problem associated only with professional athletes, recent reports estimate that 5 percent to 12 percent of male high school students and 1 percent of female students have used anabolic steroids by the time they were seniors. Concerns over a growing illicit market and prevalence of abuse combined with the possibility of harmful long-term effects of steroid use, led Congress in 1991 to place anabolic steroids into Schedule III of the Controlled Substances Act (CSA).

The CSA defines anabolic steroids as any drug or hormonal substance chemically and pharmacologically related to testosterone (other than estrogens, progestins, and corticosteroids), that promotes muscle growth. Most illicit anabolic steroids are sold at gyms, competitions and through mail order operations. For the most part, these substances are smuggled into this country. Those commonly encountered on the illicit market include: boldenone (Equipoise), ethylestrenol (Maxibolin), fluoxymesterone (Halotestin), methandriol, methandrostenolone (Dianabol), methyltestosterone, nandrolone (Durabolin, Deca-Durabolin), oxandrolone (Anavar), oxymetholone (Anadrol), stanozolol (Winstrol), testosterone and trenbolone (Finajet). In addition, a number of bogus or counterfeit products are sold as anabolic steroids.

A limited number of anabolic steroids have been approved for medical and veterinary use. The primary legitimate use of these drugs in humans is for the replacement of inadequate levels of testosterone resulting from a reduction or absence of functioning testes. In veterinary practice, anabolic steroids are used to promote feed efficiency and to improve weight gain, vigor and hair coat. They are also used in veterinary practice to treat anemia and counteract tissue breakdown during illness and trauma.

When used in combination with exercise training and high protein diet, anabolic steroids can promote increased size and strength of muscles, improve endurance and decrease recovery time between workouts. They are taken orally or by intramuscular injection. Users concerned about drug tolerance often take steroids on a schedule called a cycle. A cycle is a period of between 6 and 14 weeks of steroid use followed by a period of abstinence or reduction in use. Additionally, users tend to "stack" the drugs, using multiple drugs concurrently. Although the benefits of these practices are unsubstantiated, most users feel that cycling and stacking enhance the efficiency of the drugs and limit their side effects.

Yet another mode of steroid use is "pyramiding" in which users slowly escalate steroid use (increasing the number of drugs used at one time and/or the dose and frequency of one or more steroids) reaching a peak amount at mid-cycle and gradually tapering the dose toward the end of the cycle. The escalation of steroid use can vary with different types of training. Body builders and weight lifters tend to escalate their dose to a much higher level than do long distance runners or swimmers.

The adverse effects of large doses of multiple anabolic steroids are not well established. However, there is increasing evidence of serious health problems associated with the abuse of these agents, including cardiovascular damage; liver damage and damage to reproductive Physical side effects include elevated blood pressure and cholesterol levels, severe acne, premature balding, reduced sexual function and testicular atrophy. In males, abnormal breast development (gynecomastia) can occur. In females, anabolic steroids have a mas culinizing effect resulting in more body hair, a deeper voice, smaller breasts and fewer menstrual cycles. Several of these effects are irreversible. In adolescents, abuse of these agents may prematurely stop the lengthening of bones resulting in stunted growth.

RELATED TOPICS

CLANDESTINE LABS

Drugs of abuse in the United States come from a variety of sources. Heroin and cocaine, for example, are produced in foreign countries and smuggled into the U.S. Marijuana is cultivated domestically or smuggled from foreign sources. Legitimate pharmaceuticals are diverted to the illicit market. Continuing efforts on the part of state and federal governments to reduce the amount of dangerous and illicit drugs available for abuse, combined with the demand for psychoactive substances, have contributed to the proliferation of clandestine laboratories.

Clandestine laboratories are illicit operations consisting of chemicals and equipment necessary to manufacture controlled substances. The types and numbers of laboratories seized, to a large degree, reflect regional and national trends in the types and amounts of illicit substances that are being manufactured, trafficked and abused. Clandestine laboratories have been found in remote locations like mountain cabins and rural farms. Laboratories are also being operated in single and multifamily residences in urban and suburban neighborhoods where their toxic and explosive fumes can pose a significant threat to the health and safety of local residents.

The production of some substances, such as methamphetamine, PCP, MDMA and methcathinone, requires little sophisticated equipment or knowledge of chemistry; the synthesis of other drugs such as fentanyl and LSD requires much higher levels of expertise and equipment. Some clandestine laboratory operators have little or no training in chemistry and follow underground recipes; others employ chemistry students or professionals as "cooks."

The clandestine production of all drugs is dependent on the availability of essential raw materials. The distribution, sale, import and export of certain chemicals which are important to the manufacture of common illicitly produced substances have been regulated since the enactment of the Chemical Diversion and Trafficking Act of 1988. Enforcement of this and similar state laws has had a significant impact on the availability of chemicals to the clandestine laboratory.

INHALANTS

Inhalants are a chemically diverse group of psychoactive substances composed of organic solvents and volatile substances commonly found in adhesives, lighter fluids, cleaning fluids and paint products. Their easy accessibility, low cost and ease of concealment make inhalants, for many, one of the first substances abused. While not regulated under the CSA, a few states place restrictions on the sale of these products to minors. Studies have indicated that between 5 percent and 15 percent of young people in the United States have tried inhalants, although the vast majority of these youngsters do not become chronic abusers.

Inhalants may be sniffed directly from an open container or "huffed" from a rag soaked in the substance and held to the face. Alternatively, the open container or soaked rag can be placed in a bag where the vapors can concentrate before being inhaled. Although inhalant abusers may prefer one particular substance because of odor or taste, a variety of substances may be used because of their similar effects, availability and cost. Once inhaled, the extensive capillary surface of the lungs allows rapid absorption of the substance and blood levels peak rapidly. Entry into the brain is so fast that the effects of inhalation can resemble the intensity of effects produced by intravenous injection of other psychoactive drugs.

The effects of inhalant intoxication resemble those of alcohol inebriation, with stimulation and loss of inhibition followed by depression at high doses. Users report distortion in perceptions of time and space. Many users experience headache, nausea or vomiting, slurred speech, loss of motor coordination and wheezing. A characteristic "glue sniffer's rash" around the nose and mouth may be seen. An odor of paint or solvents on clothes, skin and breath is sometimes a sign of inhalant abuse.

The chronic use of inhalants has been associated with a number of serious health problems. Glue and paint thinner sniffing in particular produce kidney abnormalities, while the solvents, toluene and trichloroethylene, cause liver toxicity. Memory impairment, attention deficits and diminished non-verbal intelligence have been associated with the abuse of inhalants. Deaths resulting from heart failure, asphyxiation or aspiration have occurred.

———

Controlled Substances

Drugs	CSA Schedules	Trade or Other Names	Medical Uses
Narcotics			
Heroin	I	Diacetylmorphine, Horse, Smack	None in U.S., Analgesic, Antitussive
Morphine	II	Duramorph, MS-Contin, Roxanol, Oramorph SR	Analgesic
Codeine	II,III,V	Tylenol w/Codeine, Empirin w/Codeine, Robitussin A-C, Fiorinal w/Codeine, APAP w/Codeine	Analgesic, Antitussive
Hydrocodone	II,III	Tussionex, Vicodin, Hycodan, Lorcet	Analgesic, Antitussive
Hydromorphone	II	Dilaudid	Analgesic
Oxycodone	II	Percodan, Percocet, Tylox, Roxicet, Roxicodone	Analgesic
Methadone and LAAM	I,II	Dolophine, Methadose, Levo-alpha-acetylmethadol, Levomethadyl acetate	Analgesic, Treatment of Dependence
Fentanyl and Analogs	I,II	Innovar, Sublimaze, Alfenta, Sufenta, Duragesic	Analgesic, Adjunct to Anesthesia, Anesthetic
Other Narcotics	II,III,IV,V	Percodan, Percocet, Tylox, Opium, Darvon, Talwin [2], Buprenorphine, Meperidine (Pethidine), Demerol	Analgesic, Antidiarrheal
Depressants			
Chloral Hydrate	IV	Noctec, Somnos, Felsules	Hypnotic
Barbiturates	II,III,IV	Amytal, Florinal, Nembutal, Seconal, Tuinal, Phenobarbital, Pentobarbital	Anesthetic, anticonvulsant, sedative hypnotic, veterinary euthanasia agent
Benzodiazepines	IV	Ativan, Dalmane, Diazepam, Librium, Xanax, Serax, Valium, Tranxene, Verstran, Versed, Halcion, Paxipam, Restoril	Antianxiety, sedative, anticonvulsant, hypnotic
Glutethimide	II	Doriden	Sedative, hypnotic
Other Depressants	I,II,III,IV	Equanil, Miltown, Noludar, Placidyl, Valmid, Methaqualone	Antianxiety, Sedative, Hypnotic
Stimulants			
Cocaine [1]	II	Coke, Flake, Snow, Crack	Local anesthetic
Amphetamine/Methamphetamine	II	Biphetamine, Desoxyn, Dexedrine, Obetrol, Ice	Attention deficit disorder, narcolepsy, weight control
Methylphenidate	II	Ritalin	Attention deficit disorder, narcolepsy
Other Stimulants	I,II,III,IV	Adipex, Didrex, Ionamin, Melfiat, Plegine, Captagon, Sanorex, Tenuate, Tepanil, Prelu-2, Preludin	Weight control
Cannabis			
Marijuana	I	Pot, Acapulco Gold, Grass, Reefer, Sinsemilla, Thai Sticks	None
Tetrahydrocannabinol	I,II	THC, Marinol	Antinauseant
Hashish and Hashish Oil	I	Hash, Hash oil	None
Hallucinogens			
LSD	I	Acid, Microdot	None
Mescaline and Peyote	I	Mescal, Buttons, Cactus	None
Amphetamine Variants	I	2, 5-DMA, STP, MDA, MDMA, Ecstasy, DOM, DOB	None
Phencyclidine and Analogs	I,II	PCE, PCPy, TCP, PCP, Hog, Loveboat, Angel Dust	None
Other Hallucinogens	I	Bufotenine, Ibogaine, DMT, DET, Psilocybin, Psilocyn	None
Anabolic Steroids			
Testosterone (Cypionate, Enanthate)	III	Depo-Testosterone, Delatestryl	Hypogonadism
Nandrolone (Decanoate, Phenpropionate)	III	Nortestosterone, Durabolin, Deca-Durabolin, Deca	Anemia, breast cancer
Oxymetholone	III	Anadrol-50	Anemia

Uses and Effects

U.S. Department of Justice
Drug Enforcement Administration

Physical Dependence	Psychological Dependence	Tolerance	Duration (Hours)	Usual Method	Possible Effects	Effects of Overdose	Withdrawal Syndome
High	High	Yes	3-6	Injected, sniffed, smoked	● Euphoria ● Drowsiness ● Respiratory depression ● Constricted pupils ● Nausea	● Slow and shallow breathing ● Clammy skin ● Convulsions ● Coma ● Possible death	● Watery eyes ● Runny nose ● Yawning ● Loss of appetite ● Irritability ● Tremors ● Panic ● Cramps ● Nausea ● Chills and sweating
High	High	Yes	3-6	Oral, smoked, injected			
Moderate	Moderate	Yes	3-6	Oral, injected			
High	High	Yes	3-6	Oral			
High	High	Yes	3-6	Oral, injected			
High	High	Yes	4-5	Oral			
High	High	Yes	12-72	Oral, injected			
High	High	Yes	.10-72	Injected, Trans-dermal patch			
High-Low	High-Low	Yes	Variable	Oral, injected			
Moderate	Moderate	Yes	5-8	Oral	● Slurred speech ● Disorientation ● Drunken behavior without odor of alcohol	● Shallow respiration ● Clammy skin ● Dilated pupils ● Weak and rapid pulse ● Coma ● Possible death	● Anxiety ● Insomnia ● Tremors ● Delirium ● Convulsions ● Possible death
High-Mod.	High-Mod.	Yes	1-16	Oral, injected			
Low	Low	Yes	4-8	Oral, injected			
High	Moderate	Yes	4-8	Oral			
Moderate	Moderate	Yes	4-8	Oral			
Possible	High	Yes	1-2	Sniffed, smoked, injected	● Increased alertness ● Excitation ● Euphoria ● Increased pulse rate & blood pressure ● Insomnia ● Loss of appetite	● Agitation ● Increased body temperature ● Hallucinations ● Convulsions ● Possible death	● Apathy ● Long periods of sleep ● Irritability ● Depression ● Disorientation
Possible	High	Yes	2-4	Oral, injected, smoked			
Possible	High	Yes	2-4	Oral, injected			
Possible	High	Yes	2-4	Oral, injected			
Unknown	Moderate	Yes	2-4	Smoked, oral	● Euphoria ● Relaxed inhibitions ● Increased appetite ● Disorientation	● Fatigue ● Paranoia ● Possible psychosis	● Occasional reports of insomnia ● Hyperactivity ● Decreased appetite
Unknown	Moderate	Yes	2-4	Smoked, oral			
Unknown	Moderate	Yes	2-4	Smoked, oral			
None	Unknown	Yes	8-12	Oral	● Illusions and hallucinations, ● Altered perception of time and distance	● Longer ● More intensed "trip" episodes ● Psychosis ● Possible death	● Unknown
None	Unknown	Yes	8-12	Oral			
Unknown	Unknown	Yes	Variable	Oral, injected			
Unknown	High	Yes	Days	Oral, smoked			
None	Unknown	Possible	Variable	Smoked, oral, injected, sniffed			
Unknown	Unknown	Unknown	14-28 days	Injected	● Virilization ● Acne ● Testicular atrophy ● Gynecomastia ● Agressive behavior ● Edema	● Unknown	● Possible depression
Unknown	Unknown	Unknown	14-21 days	Injected			
Unknown	Unknown	Unknown	24	Oral			

Designated a narcotic under the CSA   ² Not designated a narcotic under the CSA

DEPRESSANTS

Schedule II

Trade Name:
Amytal Sodium
Controlled Ingredient:
amobarbital sodium
200 mg

Trade Name:
Doriden
Controlled Ingredient:
glutethimide
500 mg

Trade Name:
Nembutal Sodium
Controlled Ingredient:
pentobarbital sodium
100 mg

Trade Name:
Seconal Sodium
Controlled Ingredient:
secobarbital sodium
100 mg

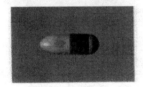

Trade Name:
Tuinal
Controlled Ingredients:
amobarbital sodium 100 mg
secobarbital sodium 100 mg

Schedule IV

Trade Name:
Ativan
Controlled Ingredient:
lorazepam
0.5 mg

Trade Name:
Ativan
Controlled Ingredient:
lorazepam
1 mg

Trade Name:
Ativan
Controlled Ingredient:
lorazepam
2 mg

Trade Name:
Centrax
Controlled Ingredient:
prazepam
5 mg

Trade Name:
Centrax
Controlled Ingredient:
prazepam 10 mg

Trade Name:
Centrax
Controlled Ingredient:
prazepam 10 mg

Trade Name:
Chloral Hydrate
Controlled Ingredient:
chloral hydrate
500 mg

Trade Name:
Dalmane
Controlled Ingredient:
flurazepam hydrochloride
15 mg

Trade Name:
Dalmane
Controlled Ingredient:
flurazepam hydrochloride
30 mg

Trade Name:
Equanil
Controlled Ingredient:
meprobamate
200 mg

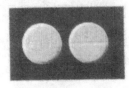

Trade Name:
Equanil
Controlled Ingredient:
meprobamate
400 mg

Trade Name:
Halcion
Controlled Ingredient:
triazolam
0.25 mg

Trade Name:
Halcion
Controlled Ingredient:
triazolam
0.5 mg

Trade Name:
Restoril
Controlled Ingredient:
temazepam
15 mg

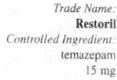

Trade Name:
Librium
Controlled Ingredient:
chlordiazepoxide hydrochloride
5 mg

Trade Name:
Restoril
Controlled Ingredient:
temazepam
30 mg

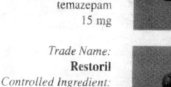

Trade Name:
Librium
Controlled Ingredient:
chlordiazepoxide hydrochloride
10 mg

Trade Name:
Serax
Controlled Ingredient:
oxazepam
10 mg

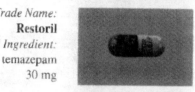

Trade Name:
Librium
Controlled Ingredient:
chlordiazepoxide hydrochloride
25 mg

Trade Name:
Serax
Controlled Ingredient:
oxazepam
15 mg

Trade Name:
Miltown 400
Controlled Ingredient:
meprobamate
400 mg

Trade Name:
Serax
Controlled Ingredient:
oxazepam 15 mg

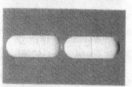

Trade Name:
Miltown 600
Controlled Ingredient:
meprobamate
600 mg

Trade Name:
Serax
Controlled Ingredient:
oxazepam
30 mg

Trade Name:
Placidyl
Controlled Ingredient:
ethchlorvynol
200 mg

Trade Name:
Tranxene
Controlled Ingredient:
clorazepate dipotassium
3.75 mg

Trade Name:
Placidyl
Controlled Ingredient:
ethchlorvynol
500 mg

Trade Name:
Tranxene
Controlled Ingredient:
clorazepate dipotassium
7.5 mg

Trade Name:
Placidyl
Controlled Ingredient:
ethchlorvynol
750 mg

Trade Name:
Tranxene
Controlled Ingredient:
clorazepate dipotassium
15 mg

Trade Name:
Valium
Controlled Ingredient:
diazepam
2 mg

Trade Name:
Valium
Controlled Ingredient:
diazepam
5 mg

Trade Name:
Valium
Controlled Ingredient:
diazepam
10 mg

Trade Name:
Xanax
Controlled Ingredient:
alprazolam
0.25 mg

Trade Name:
Xanax
Controlled Ingredient:
alprazolam
0.5 mg

Trade Name:
Xanax
Controlled Ingredient:
alprazolam
1 mg

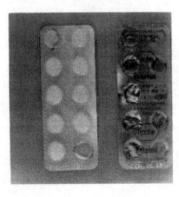

Rohyphnol contains the controlled ingredient flunitrazepam hydrochloride. Pictured here is a 2-mg tablet with packaging. "Roofies," as they are known on the street, are sold inexpensively in Mexico. They are smuggled into the United States where they have recently become a problem among American teens. The problem is rapidly spreading from the American southwest to other parts of the United States.

Trade Name:
Valium
Controlled Ingredient:
diazepam
2 mg

Trade Name:
Valium
Controlled Ingredient:
diazepam
5 mg

Trade Name:
Valium
Controlled Ingredient:
diazepam
10 mg

Trade Name:
Xanax
Controlled Ingredient:
alprazolam
0.25 mg

Trade Name:
Xanax
Controlled Ingredient:
alprazolam
0.5 mg

Trade Name:
Xanax
Controlled Ingredient:
alprazolam
1 mg

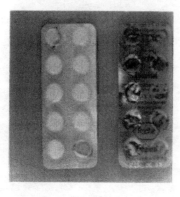

Rohyphnol contains the controlled ingredient flunitrazepam hydrochloride. Pictured here is a 2-mg tablet with packaging. "Roofies," as they are known on the street, are sold inexpensively in Mexico. They are smuggled into the United States where they have recently become a problem among American teens. The problem is rapidly spreading from the American southwest to other parts of the United States.